THE HCG DIET COOKBOOK

HELPING WEIGHT LOSS HAPPEN

THE HCG DIET COOKBOOK

HELPING WEIGHT LOSS HAPPEN

MELISSA BITTER

✬ DAEDALIAN PRESS

Las Vegas | NV
www.daedalianpress.com

© 2010 by Daedalian Press

Publication Data
The HCG Diet Cookbook: Helping Weight loss happen is about food, healthy eating, and contains no-fat / no-sugar recipes. A companion cookbook to Dr. Simeons' Pounds & Inches protocol / by Melissa Bitter. —1st ed.
     p. cm.
Includes index.
ISBN-13: 978-0-98259-441-4 (trade softcover)
ISBN-13: 978-0-98259-443-8 (e-book)
1. Reducing diets. 2. Recipe 3. Cookbook   I. Bitter, Melissa

Printed in the United States of America

First Printing | January 2010 | Daedalian Press | Las Vegas, Nevada

⚘ DAEDALIAN PRESS
Visit us on the web! daedalianpress.com

To my parents,
without whom I would
never have begun this project.

Contents

Introduction

Many people struggle with finding a diet that works for them. I have a friend in her late 50's who's tried all sorts of diets during her lifetime with mixed results. More recently, she attempted to lose weight through regular exercise but saw very little weight loss. She'd almost given up and had decided that she'd never be able shed her excess weight when she heard about the HCG diet.

The next day she called up a nurse practitioner at a health clinic she visits and a few days later, she'd begun the HCG diet. 40 days later, she'd shed 25 lbs and she's been able to keep it off.

My personal feelings are that the HCG diet is the diet that people try when all the others have failed. It's obscure, most people haven't heard about it. It's extreme, restricting yourself to very few calories. And it's a little crazy, taking the HCG hormone either through injection or homeopathically.

But here's the key and this is the only thing that matters, the diet works.

For reasons of your own you also have chosen to go the HCG route. I'm happy you've heard about the diet and I wish you the best success on your journey. May your dreams, like my friend's, come true!

My intent and purpose in writing this book was to help you along this journey by creating recipes that you'd enjoy. Since real hunger is nonexistent when you're taking the HCG hormone, I want your meals to be enjoyable and thoroughly satisfying. I want to help you see options as you return to the kitchen, so that the first phase will pass more quickly and easily than you expected.

Your diet will go so much better than you dreamed, because you're going to enjoy the food *and* lose the weight.

On a side note, I did not write this book as a strict 100 grams this and 20mg's that. It's a straightforward approach to down to earth and tasty cooking.

Familiarize yourself with Dr. Simeons' *Pounds & Inches* (you can find it online) and keep to his list of approved food items. Then eat the following things each day: two servings of protein, two fruits, two starches, and four vegetables. (Yes I said four, you can thank me later.) My friend's nurse practitioner recommends four vegetables a day.

She also said that her clients see a lot of success on the diet if they ingested one tablespoon of agave every day. Do with that what you will. That's it. Oh, and drink your water, 1 oz for ever 2 lbs you weigh.

-Melissa

What & Why

I can only guess at why Dr. Simeons included the following fruits & vegetables, and not others, on his diet, but this much I know, his choices are nutritional powerhouses, providing minerals and nutrients that help our bodies run just right.

I added the What & Why section to help us learn a little more about these fruits and vegetables. My intent is that we become more comfortable using them in our every day cooking. As a bonus, I've added a spices section. There are so many wonderful flavors, the combinations are endless.

Think of these next few pages as an introductory guide into a fantastic world of cooking. Use your imagination and try things out, enjoy, and most of all, have fun!

-Melissa

Protein

Beef

HAVE you ever strolled down the meat section of the grocery store and thrown your hands up in frustration? Well, you're not alone.

There are more than 300 cuts of beef, and around 1,000 different names that correspond to those cuts. Each cut tastes, cooks, and is seasoned differently. For instance some have a gamey taste; others are light and delicious; require long cooking times; do best when marinated; are marbled with fat (not such a bad thing, except while on this diet); or are best when cut up into chunks for kabobs or stews.

But don't worry about all of this. As you begin to cook, you'll discover which cuts you like best and how to prepare them. Cooking is a matter of discovery, of trial and error as you taste your way into a new lifestyle.

For the immediate future don't worry about searching for specific types of meat, simply rely on a visual check. Study the meat and select cuts that have the least amount of fat running through them (This fat is called marbling, and it gives the meat flavor and tenderness.) Look for cuts that are as solid red as possible. Any fat on the edges is easy to trim off, so focus on the center part of the cut.

For reference, the leanest cuts are Top Sirloin, Bottom Round Roast, Top Round, Mock Tender, and Eye of Round Roast. If you need ground beef, stick with ground Sirloin. After the diet, try out ground Chuck for better flavor.

Beef is a good source of Riboflavin, Niacin and Zinc, and a very good source of Protein, Vitamin C, Vitamin B12, Iron, Phosphorus, Copper and Selenium.

Look for cuts of beef that are red and fresh looking. Avoid beef that is dull or gray, or has turned brown.

Nutrition: 3.5 oz raw, 161 calories, 1.4 fat, 55mg Cholesterol, 38mg Sodium, 0g Total Carbs, 0g Fiber, 0g Sugar, 29.1g Protein, 6mg Calcium, 237.1mg Potassium

Chicken

CHICKEN breasts are fairly universal. Your best bet when purchasing chicken is to look for fresh, skinless, and boneless breasts.

The main thing to be careful of when buying is the supplier. Some fresh, unfrozen chicken breasts have been pumped full of saline to make the meat plumper. Of course the water cooks out, leaving you with a saltier, more expensive piece of meat. The other decision to make is whether to go free-range or not.

It is said that free-range chicken not only tastes better, but that it is more nutritious. Plus, the steroid-free meat is nicer to your system. The decision comes down to cost; if you can afford it, try it. You might like it.

Chicken is a good source of Vitamin B6 and Phosphorus, and a very good source of Protein, Niacin and Selenium.

Look for boneless, skinless chicken breasts that have a nice pink color and smooth creamy skin. Avoid chicken that looks dry, has visible tears, bruises, is turning gray, or smells rancid.

Nutrition: 3.5 oz raw, 109 calories, 1.2 fat, 58mg Cholesterol, 64mg Sodium, 0g Total Carbs, 0g Fiber, 0g Sugar, 22.9g Protein, 10.9mg Calcium, 253mg Potassium

Crab

CRAB meat has a relatively mild taste, is succulent and sweet. Purchase it already flaked apart, frozen (crab legs), or live if you like living on the wild side. Watch out for lower grade crab, because it will taste briny.

It is a good source of Vitamin C, Folate and Magnesium, and a very good source of Protein, Vitamin B12, Phosphorus, Zinc, Copper and Selenium.

Look for crab that smells fresh and is free from gray splotches. If buying fresh, avoid crab that has a fishy or ammonia smell.

Nutrition: 3.5 oz raw, 83 calories, 0.6 fat, 42mg Cholesterol, 830mg Sodium, 0g Total Carbs, 0g Fiber, 0g Sugar, 18.1g Protein, 45.6mg Calcium, 202.4mg Potassium

White Fish

SEVERAL fish types fit under this category: Tuna, Orange Roughy, and Tilapia to name a few. Pan sear it, broil it, or grill it. Throw it into a fish soup, or make it into a salad to top a Wasa cracker.

Although the nutrient value of each fish is different, white fish is generally a good source of Niacin and Phosphorus, and a very good source of Protein, Vitamin B12 and Selenium.

Look for fish that is firm, springs back when you poke it, and smells like fresh salt water. Avoid fish that has an overly fishy, ammonia-like smell.

Breakdown is for Orange Roughy.
Nutrition: 3.5 oz raw, 75 calories, 0.7 fat, 60mg Cholesterol, 71mg Sodium, 0g Total Carbs, 0g Fiber, 0g Sugar, 16.3g Protein, 8.9mg Calcium, 165.7mg Potassium

Lobster

IF purchasing frozen, allow your lobster tail to un-thaw completely in the refrigerator. If you cook it before it's thawed the meat will turn tough.

To deshell a lobster with a pair of scissors, cut down the center of the back shell. To remove the uncooked flesh, run a finger between the meat and the shell to loosen them from each other, then lift the uncooked tail out of the shell.

Tip: use your discarded lobster shells to make a broth to season your vegetables.

It is a good source of Vitamin B12, Pantothenic Acid and Phosphorus, and a very good source of Protein, Zinc, Copper and Selenium.

Look for cold water lobster, as their flesh is (more reliably) firmer and of better quality. Avoid lobster that has a fishy, ammonia like smell, that has gray spots on the flesh, or a grayish cast to the tail.

Nutrition: 3.5 oz raw, 89 calories, 0.9 fat, 94mg Cholesterol, 294mg Sodium, 0.5g Total Carbs, 0g Fiber, 0g Sugar, 18.7g Protein, 47.6mg Calcium, 272.9mg Potassium

Shrimp

THERE are over 300 species of shrimp. Although similar in taste, they vary in size, texture, and flavor. Wild shrimp swim freely so their meat is firmer than their farm-bred cousins. They also have thicker shells and richer flavor. Shrimp spoils quickly, so if you buy it unfrozen, eat it within a day of purchase.

Shrimp cooks quickly. When it's pink, it's done. Don't overcook them otherwise they'll lose their sweet, delicate flavor and turn rubbery. They can be steamed, grilled, boiled, sautéed, baked, or deep-fried, with or without the shell, and with or without the vein.

The vein on shrimp is it's digestive track. It's up to you whether you want to remove it or not. My preference is to remove it.   Simply pull off the shell, then run a pairing knife along the back of the shrimp. Cut shallowly, just enough to either pull or rinse the vein out of the shrimp.

FYI: Shrimp are easier to devein before cooking.

Shrimp are a good source of Niacin, Iron, Phosphorus and Zinc, and a very good source of Protein, Vitamin B12 and Selenium.

Look for shrimp that are gray and almost translucent. Avoid shrimp that smell of anything other than salt-water, or have black spots or stripes (unless they're Tiger Shrimp, which are black-striped).

Nutrition: 3.5 oz raw, 105 calories, 0.3 fat, 151mg Cholesterol, 147mg Sodium, 0.9g Total Carbs, 0g Fiber, 0g Sugar, 20.2g Protein, 51.6mg Calcium, 183.6mg Potassium

Fruit

Apple

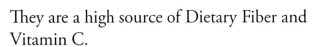

THERE are over 2,000 known varieties of apples grown in the US, and more than 7,500 grown world-wide. The most common varieties range from tart (Granny Smith) to sugary sweet (Golden Delicious). They add crunchy sweetness to salads and are frequently paired with cinnamon.

They are a high source of Dietary Fiber and Vitamin C.

Look for firm, shiny, smooth-skinned apples with intact stems. Avoid apples that are wrinkled, mushy, or have soft spots.

Nutrition: 1 medium apple, 95 calories, 0.1 fat, 0 Cholesterol, 2mg Sodium 25.1g Total Carbs, 4.4g Fiber, 18.9g Sugar, 0.5g Protein, 10.9mg Calcium 194.7mg Potassium

Strawberry

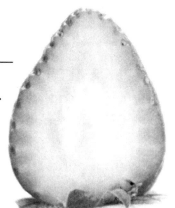

STRAWBERRIES range from tart to sweet. Slice them on a spinach salad, make them into a sauce, or blend them into a smoothie or dessert.

They are a good source of Folate and Potassium, and are a very good source of Dietary Fiber, Vitamin C and Manganese.

Look for strawberries that are dark red in color, bright, and are firm and shiny. Avoid strawberries that are shriveled, moldy, or too soft.

Nutrition: 6 medium strawberries, 23 calories, 0.1 fat, 0 Cholesterol 1mg Sodium, 5.5g Total Carbs, 1.4g Fiber, 3.4g Sugar, 0.5g Protein, 11.5mg Calcium, 110.2mg Potassium

Grapefruit

GRAPEFRUIT have a tangy sweet flavor and are very juicy. They range from white to pinkish red inside, and can be very sweet or tart depending on the variety.

They are a good source of Dietary Fiber, Vitamin A and Potassium, and are a very good source of Vitamin C.

Look for grapefruit that are firm and heavy for their size with smooth even colored skin. Avoid grapefruit that are misshapen, shriveled, or have brown spots.

Nutrition: ½ grapefruit, 20 calories, 0.1 fat, 0 Cholesterol, 0mg Sodium, 5.2g Total Carbs, 0.7g Fiber, 4.5g Sugar, 0.4g Protein, 7.7mg Calcium, 89mg Potassium

Lemon

LEMONS have a bright, clear, and tart flavor. They enhance both sweet and savory sauces and dishes. Squeeze fresh juice over steamed vegetables, grilled chicken or fish, or on a salad seasoned lightly with salt and pepper. Lemon peel can be used when grated or zested.

They are a good source of Thiamin, Riboflavin, Pantothenic Acid, Iron and Magnesium, and a very good source of Dietary Fiber, Vitamin B6 & C, Calcium, Potassium and Copper.

Look for lemons that are firm with smooth, bright yellow colored skin. Avoid lemons that are too soft, too hard, wrinkled or are mushy.

Nutrition: 1 lemon, 24 calories, 0.3 fat, 0 Cholesterol, 2mg Sodium, 7.8g Total Carbs, 2.4g Fiber, 2.1g Sugar, 0.9g Protein, 21.8mg Calcium, 115.9mg Potassium

Lime

LIMES are my go-to citrus of choice for seasoning soups, vegetables, and meats. They are a bit more sharp than lemons and I like how they cut through the flavor in many of my favorite dishes.

They can be used in everything from drinks and vinaigrettes to baked dishes. Try adding lime juice to a fresh tomato salsa, or squeezing one over freshly grilled seafood. It will add a lightness and roundness to a bowl of chicken soup. Try lime zest in a vinaigrette or marinade for a stronger lime flavor.

They are a good source of Calcium, Iron and Copper, and a very good source of Dietary Fiber and Vitamin C.

Look for limes that are dark green in color with smooth skin that yields to gentle pressure. Avoid limes that are too hard, too soft, or that are wrinkled.

Nutrition: 1 lime, 20 calories, 0.1 fat, 0 Cholesterol, 1mg Sodium, 7.0g Total Carbs, 1.9g Fiber, 1.1g Sugar, 0.5g Protein, 22.1mg Calcium, 68.3mg Potassium

Vegetables

Asparagus

ASPARAGUS has a sweet full, yet delicate flavor that reminds me of spring. It comes in a few varieties: dark green, dark green with purplish tips, purple, and white.

Tip: the woody part of an asparagus stem will snap off with a little pressure. Discard or use them to season a vegetable broth.

It is one of those wonderful well-balanced vegetables. Not only is it a good source of Potassium, Dietary Fiber, Vitamins A, B6, C & K, and Thiamin. It also produces more Glutathione and Folic Acid than any other vegetable.

Look for dark green, fresh stalks, the thicker the better, with tight tips. Avoid slimy, wilted or stringy looking stalks.

Nutrition: 1 cup raw, 27 calories, 0.1 fat, 0 Cholesterol, 3mg Sodium 5.2g Total Carbs, 2.8g Fiber, 2.5g Sugar, 2.9g Protein, 32.2mg Calcium, 270.7mg Potassium

Beet Greens

BEET GREENS have a lively bitter taste, similar to chard. Sauté or steam them then spritz with a little lemon juice, or add to a soup.

They are highly nutritious, providing Protein, Calcium, Dietary Fiber, Vitamins A, B6 & C, Magnesium, Copper, Potassium, and Beta-carotene & Lutein (both cartenoids).

Look for dark green leaves that are crisp and bright, with rich red veins and fairly long upright stalks. Avoid bunches that are wilted, yellowed, or slimy.

Nutrition: 1 cup raw, 8 calories, 0 fat, 0 Cholesterol, 86mg Sodium, 1.6g Total Carbs, 1.4g Fiber, 0.2g Sugar, 0.8g Protein, 44.5mg Calcium, 289.6mg Potassium

Cabbage

CABBAGE comes in several varieties: green, red, napa, and chinese (also known as bok choy). It has a tart tanginess, pleasing aroma, and makes a colorful and crunchy addition to salads, stir fries, casseroles, soups and stews. It can be turned into sauerkraut, which in turn is a great side dish to beef.

It contains Protein and is an excellent source of Vitamins B6, C & K, Folate, Magnesium, Calcium and Potassium.

Look for firm heads of cabbage, that are dense with crisp, shiny, colorful leaves. Avoid heads that have cracked leaves, bruises, and blemishes.

Nutrition: 1 cup raw, 17 calories, 0.1 fat, 0 Cholesterol, 13mg Sodium, 3.9g Total Carbs, 1.4g Fiber, 2.4g Sugar, 1g Protein, 32.9mg Calcium, 172.2mg Potassium

Celery

CELERY is crunchy, has a deep clean taste and is a great snack. It gives an herby backbone to soups and stews, and a bit of crunch to salads.

It's a good source of Dietary Fiber, Iron, Vitamins A, B & C, and Potassium, and is the best vegetable source of naturally occurring Sodium.

Look for even colored, heavy, firm, and thick medium green stalks of celery. This will yield a nice mild flavor. Sniff the celery, the stronger the scent, the stronger the flavor. FYI: Dark green stalks tend to be tougher and stringier. Avoid white stalks that are limp, yellowing, or floppy.

Nutrition: 1 cup raw, 14 calories, 0.2 fat, 0 Cholesterol, 81mg Sodium, 3.4g Total Carbs, 1.6g Fiber, 1.8g Sugar, 0.7g Protein, 40.4mg Calcium, 262.6mg Potassium

Chard

CHARD is similar in flavor to beet greens and spinach, with a sweet yet bitter, slightly salty flavor. Tall with big leaves, it comes in green, red and yellow varieties. It can be eaten raw (although it's slightly bitter), sautéed or steamed, and makes a nice addition to soups.

It has exceptional health promoting nutrients, and is an excellent source of Vitamins A, C & K, as well as Magnesium, Manganese, Potassium, Iron, and is a good source of Vitamins B2, B6 & E, Copper, Calcium, and Dietary Fiber.

Look for leaves that are vivid in color, crisp and unblemished. Avoid leaves that have brown or yellow spots, are slimy or wilting, or that have tiny holes.

Nutrition: 1 cup raw, 7 calories, 0.1 fat, 0 Cholesterol, 77mg Sodium, 1.3g Total Carbs, 0.6g Fiber, 0.4g Sugar, 0.6g Protein, 18.4mg Calcium, 136.4mg Potassium

Chicory

CHICORY is also known as endive, which is available in two varieties. The first is called radicchio, a compact head of red leaves. The second, called frisee, is a loose head of curly leaves that are dark green on the tips and white toward the center. Both have similar tastes, but different textures.

The delicate texture and bitter flavor of frisee chicory makes it perfect for warm salads. Try it with lemon tarragon dressing or toss the white crunchy parts of chicory into a soup just moments before you pull it off the stove.

Chicory is a good source of Vitamins E, A, C & K, dietary fiber, Thiamin, Riboflavin, Folate, Pantothenic Acid, Calcium, Iron, Potassium, Zinc, Copper, and Manganese.

Look for crisp heads. Avoid heads that look wilted.

Nutrition: 1 cup raw, 7 calories, 0.1 fat, 0 Cholesterol, 13mg Sodium, 1.4g Total Carbs, 1.2g Fiber, 0.2g Sugar, 0.5g Protein, 29mg Calcium, 121.8mg Potassium

Cucumber

CUCUMBERS are fresh tasting and add texture and crunch to a salad. They have a cooling effect on the mouth and compliment hot spicy dishes. Eat them with the peel on, either sliced, grated, or chopped. Try adding cucumbers to a smoothie for a light vegetable accent. The two most popular varieties are Green Cucumbers and English Cucumbers. I like both, but prefer English Cucumbers because they are less watery, and the seeds are practically non-existent.

They are a very good source of Vitamin C & A, Potassium, Manganese, Folate, Dietary Fiber, Magnesium, and Silica.

Look for cucumbers that have an even color from medium to dark green, and are firm and rounded at their edges. Avoid cucumbers that are limp, yellow, puffy, shriveled, or soft on the ends.

Nutrition: 1 cup raw, 16 calories, 0.1 fat, 0 Cholesterol, 2mg Sodium, 3.7g Total Carbs, 0.5g Fiber, 1.7g Sugar, 0.7g Protein, 16.6mg Calcium, 152.9mg Potassium

Fennel

FENNEL is closely related to parsley, dill, and coriander. Its texture is similar to celery, and it tastes like sweet mild licorice or anise. It works great in salads, soups, and to flavor meat dishes. Try adding fennel to chicken, fish, or vegetable stocks for a new depth of flavor.

It has strong antioxidant qualities, is an excellent source of Vitamin C, and is a very good source of Fiber, Folate, and Potassium.

Look for bulbs that are clean, tight, firm, and solid; that are whitish or pale green in color and that have firm green stalks. Avoid bulbs that are split, bruised, spotted, or have signs of flowering buds.

Fennel should be stored in the refrigerator.

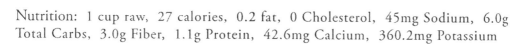

Nutrition: 1 cup raw, 27 calories, 0.2 fat, 0 Cholesterol, 45mg Sodium, 6.0g Total Carbs, 3.0g Fiber, 1.1g Protein, 42.6mg Calcium, 360.2mg Potassium

Green Salad

GREEN LEAFY VEGETABLES are a powerhouse of concentrated nutrients. They are a good source of fiber, vitamins and minerals. They range from mild tasting to spicy.

Wrap them around fish, chicken or beef to make a sandwich, or—when appropriate—sauté them with a little bit of salt and pepper, a squeeze of citrus or a splash of vinegar. Alternately you could add them to a soup or marinara sauce.

A few salad greens you might enjoy:
Arugula has a peppery flavor that works well in a salad or soup.
Dandelion Greens have a bitter, tangy flavor and are best when eaten steamed or raw.
Mustard Greens have a peppery or spicy flavor and are delicious in soups, salads, or as a side.
Watercress has a spicy flavor, and is good in soup or salad.

Look for dark green, crisp, leaves with vibrant color. Avoid leaves that are wilted, brown, yellow, or have tiny holes.

WATERCRESS

Lettuce

LETTUCE comes in many varieties. Its sweet mild flavor and crunchy texture makes it the perfect accompaniment to practically anything. Serve it with a light dressing or spritz it with and a dash of salt & freshly ground black pepper.

It is high in Vitamin A and is a good source of Folate.

Look for crisp leaves with vibrant color. Avoid heads of lettuce that are discolored, wilted, yellowed, or have brown spots.

Nutrition: 1 cup raw, 8 calories, 0.1 fat, 0 Cholesterol, 4mg Sodium, 1.6g Total Carbs, 1.0g Fiber, 0.6g Sugar, 0.6g Protein, 15.5mg Calcium, 116.1mg Potassium

Onion

ONIONS vary from mild and garlicky to
sweet and spicy. They are an essential component of many recipes, rounding out flavor or giving a little bit of a punch. They can be grilled, added to soups, sauces, salads, and salsas.

They are a good source of Chromium, Vitamin C, and Dietary Fiber.

Look for onions that are clean, well shaped, have no opening at the neck, and are firm. They can have a papery skin or not. Avoid onions that are moldy, spongy, have sprouted, and look wilted. Store at room temperature, away from bright light, in a well ventilated area.

Tip: To remove the onion smell from your hands, rub your fingers against stainless steel, while washing.

Nutrition: 1 cup raw, 48 calories, 0.1 fat, 0 Cholesterol, 3mg Sodium, 11.6g Total Carbs, 1.6g Fiber, 4.9g Sugar, 1.1g Protein, 25.3mg Calcium, 165.6mg Potassium

Types you might recognize:

Green Onions are also known as scallions. They have a mild onion flavor and crunch that works great as a garnish when sliced into skinny rings. Add them to a Pico de Gallo salsa if you want a milder onion flavor. They'll stay crisp if you cook them for only a moment, otherwise they turn limp.

Look for green onions that are green, tender and fresh. Avoid ones that are wilted and yellowish.

Red Onions have a mild, sweet flavor. Eat them raw on salads or add them to your marinara.

Shallots are mildly sharp, but are not as potent as the other onions. They turn mild when cooked, and their flavor is a cross between mild garlic and onion. They work great in sauces, vinaigrettes, and in tuna or egg salad when you want just a little crunch and flavor.

Spanish Onions are pungent and release their flavor when sautéed, grilled, or roasted, they are too strong to be eaten raw.

Sweet Onions have a naturally high sugar content. Dice them into fresh salsas or grill them to make a great side dish.

White Onions are very aromatic and flavorful. They're slightly sweeter than yellow onions but are spicy. They'll give kick to your Pico de Gallo salsa.

Yellow Onions are pungent but sweet. They are the universal cooking onion.

Radish

RADISHES come in many varieties, Daikon (white, mild), French Breakfast (deep pink with white tips, mild) or your regular radish that is bright red on the outside and white in the center. They have lots of crunch and range from mild to wildly hot and spicy (Watermelon). They are best eaten raw a little nibble at a time or sliced on a salad. They turn mild when roasted.

FYI: The spiciness of radishes is also influenced by its growing conditions. The hotter and drier the weather is, the spicier they'll be no matter the variety.

They are a good source of Riboflavin, Vitamin B6, Calcium, Magnesium, Copper, Manganese, and is a very good source of Vitamin C, Potassium and Folate.

Look for smooth, brightly colored, medium sized radishes with crisp fresh looking tops. Avoid radishes that feel soft or mushy, have brown marks, or look dull.

Nutrition: 1 cup raw, 27 calories, 0.1 fat, 0 Cholesterol, 3mg Sodium, 5.2g Total Carbs, 2.8g Fiber, 2.5g Sugar, 2.9g Protein, 32.2mg Calcium, 270.7mg Potassium

Spinach

SPINACH has a clean, crisp, sweet flavor, with a light sharpness. It works great in salads, soups, and can be steamed and sautéed. It is grown in sandy soil so wash it thoroughly.

It is high in Dietary Fiber, Vitamins A & C, Iron, Folate, and Magnesium.

Look for dark green leaves. Avoid wilted and yellowed leaves.

Nutrition: 1 cup raw, 7 calories, 0.1 fat, 0 Cholesterol, 24mg Sodium, 1.1g Total Carbs, 0.7g Fiber, 0.1g Sugar, 0.9g Protein, 29.7mg Calcium, 167.4mg Potassium

Tomato

TOMATOES are mildly sweet and acidic. They are versatile and can be used in salads, on sandwiches, as a base to a stew, soup, or sauce. Sprinkle a little balsamic vinegar over one, with some fresh basil and you've got a great treat.

They are rich in Lycopene, Flavonoids and other Phytochemicals with anticarcinogenic properties. They're high in Vitamins A & C, and are a great source of Potassium.

Look for tomatoes that have rich deep color, sweet fragrance, and are well shaped with smooth skin. Avoid tomatoes that have wrinkles, cracks, bruises, soft spots, or are puffy.

Tomatoes are sensitive to cold. Storing them in a very cold refrigerator may cause them to turn mealy and lose their flavor.

Nutrition: 1 cup raw, 32 calories, 0.1 fat, 0 Cholesterol, 9mg Sodium, 7.0g Total Carbs, 2.2g Fiber, 4.7g Sugar, 1.6g Protein, 18.0mg Calcium, 426.6mg Potassium

Types of tomatoes that you might recognize:

Beefsteak Tomatoes have a heavy flesh and are tangy, sturdy, and slightly smoky. They work great on a sandwich or burger.

Cherry Tomatoes are sweet. They're great in salads, on the grill or in a sauce.

Grape Tomatoes are tiny, firm and sweet, and have a fresh bold taste. They're perfect for salads or as a zingy snack.

Plum Tomatoes are also known as Roma tomatoes. They are tangy, sweet, and are ideal for sauces. Slow cooking brings out their roundness of flavor.

Vine Ripened Tomatoes are my favorite. They have a mild but full flavor and work great in salads, sauces, or baked dishes.

Extras

Agave

AGAVE is a natural wholesome sweetener extracted from the agave plant. It has a full sweet flavor and because it is low on the glycemic index, the body won't react with an insulin spike. When you need to add a little sweetener to something you cook, use Agave, regardless of whether you're on the HCG diet or not.

FYI: agave is sweeter than sugar, so you need less of it.

FYI II: The nurse practitioner that counselled my friend while on the HCG diet said that her clients see very good results when they ingest one tablespoon of agave everyday.

Nutrition: 1 TBSP, 60 calories, 0 fat, 0 Cholesterol, 0 Sodium, 16g Total Carbs, 0 Fiber, 16g Sugar, 0g Protein

Salt

SALT comes in many varieties, each one is used for a specific purpose.

Here are a few you might recognize and enjoy:

Kosher Salt is my go-to salt of choice. It forms a very large salt crystal while it is dried, giving it a very mild delicate flavor. Because the salt crystals are so large, don't freak out (like my mom) when you find you use more of it than you're used to.

Fleur de Sel is my second go-to salt of choice. It has a large salt crystal similar to Kosher Salt, but it dissolves slower and gives an earthy flavor to your dishes.

Pickling Salt is very fine grained and is used when making pickles or sauerkraut. It is very concentrated so use caution when substituting it for one of its cousins.

Rock Salt is most commonly used to help make ice cream. A less common use is to cook shrimp, see the recipe on pg 116.

Table Salt is my least favorite salt, but is the most common. I find that it has a slightly metallic flavor that I don't care for.

Wasa

Wasa CRACKERS come in a variety of flavors (rye, sourdough, and whole wheat to name a few), but they are all fairly similar in taste (much to my chagrin). The main difference between crackers is texture, which depends on the fiber content.

I like Wasa crackers because they provide a satisfying crunch, they're substantial, and I like the texture. You'll look forward to this daily treat.

The alternative starch for the HCG diet are Grissini, which (most likely because of the white flour) taste like candy to me. Not only are Wasa crackers more satisfying, they're healthier.

Make them your go to cracker/starch while on the HCG diet.

Nutrition: 1 cracker, 27 calories, 0.1 fat, 0 Cholesterol, 3mg Sodium, 5.2g Total Carbs, 2.8g Fiber, 2.5g Sugar, 2.9g Protein, 32.2mg Calcium, 270.7mg Potassium

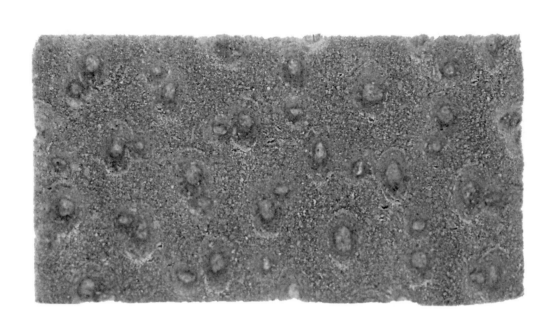

Herbs & Spices

Herbs & Spices

ALLSPICE comes from the berries of the Jamaican bayberry tree. It has a heavy sweetness, which is reminiscent of cloves, cinnamon, and nutmeg. Use the whole berries when poaching fish, making corned beef, or when pickling fruits or vegetables. Use ground allspice to season sauces and make Jamaican Jerk chicken.

BAY LEAVES can be used both fresh and dried, and is similar in taste to oregano and thyme. It comes in two varieties, the first has a soft and subtle flavor (Turkish) and the second is sharp and bitter (Californian). Try it in your soups or stews, a marinara, or when making Mediterranean or Mexican dishes. Remember, if you cook with the whole leaves, discard them after cooking.

BLACK PEPPER is the most frequently used spice. It adds depth of flavor to nearly any savory dish, and many sweet dishes as well. It comes in three varieties: black, white, and green. Green is the mildest, black has a stronger flavor, and white is the most intense. Since pepper loses its flavor as soon as it's ground, grind it as you need it using a pepper mill. Try freshly ground pepper on a salad, in a soup, or to season freshly cooked meat.

BASIL can be used both fresh and dried, and is a very common ingredient in Italian, French, Indian, and Asian cooking. It blends well with Thyme, Garlic, and Oregano, and is often paired with tomatoes. When you use fresh basil, toss it in at the end of the cooking time since its flavor will quickly cook away. If it's dried, the cook time does not matter. There are a few varieties of basil, some have hints of anise, and others are sweeter. Try dried basil with chicken and fish. Try fresh basil, with a ripe tomato and a splash of balsamic vinegar.

CARDAMOM has a strong unique flavor, is slightly sweet, and is very aromatic. In the Middle East, they use it to flavor coffee, Scandinavian countries use it in desserts, and Indian dishes feature it in their curries and spiced rice dishes. To shake things up a bit, try it with fish, meat loaf, and fish stews.

CILANTRO is best used fresh and has a citrus-sage-like aroma. Both the leaves and stems can be used. It is most commonly used in Chinese, Indian, Egyptian, Persian and Mexican dishes. I love it in fresh salsa or tossed in a soup. Its flavor will be lost if cooked, so chop or mince it up and use it as a garnish.

CINNAMON is fragrant and has a sweet and warm flavor. It is a key ingredient in Chinese Five Spice, and some Asian and Middle Eastern dishes.

CLOVES are rich, sweet and sultry. Try poking a few dozen cloves into an onion and dropping it into your stock pot. Or drop a few into your simmering apple-sauce.

CORIANDER is the seed from the cilantro plant. It has a pleasantly sweet, spicy flavor with hints of lemon. It is commonly used in chili and curry dishes, but is also used to flavor soups. It is used most often in Latin American, Middle Eastern, and Indian cooking.

CUMIN has an earthy flavor that you'll recognize from chili and fajitas. It is used most often in Latin American, Indian, and Middle Eastern cooking.

FENNEL SEED has a delicate flavor; light and sweet, similar to anise. Add ground fennel to your marinara or tomato sauce for a variation. It is often used in fish dishes. I like to use fennel seed when I make chicken soup.

GINGER can be used both fresh and dried and have noticeably different flavors. It pairs well with garlic and has a spicy edge to it. It can be used in a sauce, dressing or marinade and is often used in Asian cooking.

GARLIC is readily available in fresh or dried forms. I love it freshly minced and in its dried granulated form. Add it to practically anything to give it a rich earthy flavor.

MAJORAM has a delicate, sweet floral flavor similar to oregano, and can be used both fresh and dried. If you plan to use it fresh, add it at end of the cooking time to preserve its flavor. It is most commonly paired with basil, oregano, thyme and rosemary and is used in Italian and Mediterranean cooking.

MINT comes in a few varieties. It ranges from pungent and peppery to sweet. It is most commonly found in Greek, Turk-ish, and Middle Eastern cooking. It blends well with fruit, meats, and other herbs. Use spearmint fresh, chopped up as a garnish, or steep it in hot water to make an afternoon tea. It pairs well with lime, and other light dishes.

MUSTARD POWDER is made from small seeds that have a strong pungent flavor. Use it in marinades and vinaigrettes.

ONION POWDER, when you don't have onions on hand, or just want a hint of flavor to round out whatever you're cooking, onion powder will do the trick. Use it in marinades and dressings.

OREGANO can be used both fresh and dried, and comes in a couple varieties. Greek oregano is delicate, bright and sweet with lemony overtones that work best with Mediterranean dishes. Mexican oregano is much heartier and earthy. Oregano pairs well with basil and is often used in tomato-based dishes, and to season meat or fish.

ROSEMARY can be used both fresh and dried and is most commonly used in Mediterranean cooking. It tastes great in tomato sauces, soups or stews, and baked items. Try pairing fresh rosemary with garlic when baking chicken.

SAGE, when fresh, has grayish-green leaves. It has a robust earthy bouquet, a little like mint but musty and deep. It can be used both fresh and dried, and is most commonly used in things you shouldn't be eating when on the HCG diet. It pairs well with many of the Italian seasonings and adds flavor to salads, dressings, stews and marinades.

STAR ANISE has a strong, sweet, licorice flavor. It is used to flavor tea, marinades, and soups. It is a key ingredient in Chinese Five Spice blend and many Asian dishes. Try it in meat rubs, and bbq sauce.

TARRAGON has a bittersweet flavor that is commonly used in vinaigrettes. It can be used both fresh and dried and pairs well with chicken, fish, shrimp and other seafood.

THYME can be used both fresh and dried, and has a spicy, floral aroma. It is a versatile herb and it is frequently paired with rosemary. It is a key ingredient to Jamaican Jerk. Remove the leaves from fresh thyme sprigs by pinching the top of the stem and pulling the leaves down. Try it with rosemary and garlic when baking chicken or add it to your chicken soup.

THYME

Chilies

Dried chilies are a common ingredient in Southwestern, Asian and Latin American cooking. I like to use several different chili powders together when I cook, since each chili imparts a slightly different flavor. Some are smoky, others are sweet, and of course they range from quite mild to wildly hot. Layering them together gives a dish a rounder, more satisfying flavor.

When shopping, look for chilies that smell pungent and bright, not muted and dusty. The chipotle, california, and pasilla varieties should not look dull.

FYI: Old chilies become brittle as they age, so look for dried chilies that are relatively soft.

When working with chilies, make sure to thoroughly wash your hands after handling since the residual oils will irritate your eyes (if you happen to touch them) and skin.

Some recipes call for toasted pepper flakes (pepper flakes are crushed dried chilies). To toast pepper flakes simply preheat a skillet over medium heat, turn on your air vent to high (because the fumes coming off the pepper flakes will make your eyes burn), toss them onto the hot pan, and shake it back and forth over the heat letting the flakes slowly rotate and flip to become evenly toasted. The entire process should take between 15-30 seconds. If they smell burned, throw them out, wash your pan and start over.

These are a few of my favorites:

ANCHO chilies are the dried version of poblano peppers. They have a mild, somewhat sweet and rich flavor with medium heat (if ground with the seeds) or mild heat (if ground with no seeds). It is most recognizable in chili (the soup). Sprinkle a little over fish or use it as a great base for Mexican dishes, chili, meat rubs, and sauces.

ARBOL chilies are tiny red chilies that pack a lot of heat. Toss them into chili, salsa, stir-fries and curries. When ground into a powder, it is similar to cayenne pepper; just a pinch will give any dish just the right amount of heat.

CALIFORNIA chili powder (also known as California Paprika) is mild and sweet. It's the ideal paprika to use if you're looking for color and garnish appeal.

CAYENNE PEPPER is very hot, pungent and biting with a slightly aromatic scent. When a recipe calls for red pepper, this is the pepper it means. Just a ¼ tsp will add the zip you're looking for in a recipe.

CHILI POWDER is a blend of powdered chili peppers, cumin, garlic, and oregano.

CHIPOTLE chili powder has very mild heat and a deep smoky flavor. Chipotle peppers are actually dried, smoked jalapeño peppers. Add a dash into your soup, salsa, or side dishes.

MULATO chili powder has a smoky, licorice, and aromatic flavor. It has a very mild heat and is used mostly for its flavor.

NEW MEXICO chili powder is mildly hot, with earthy rich tones reminiscent of wild cherries. It has a sweet, pungent, earthy flavor.

HUNGARIAN PAPRIKA has a savory flavor with heat that ranges from spicy hot to mildly sweet.

SPANISH PAPRIKA has a smoky, savory flavor and is commonly found in Mediterranean and Spanish cooking. Pair it with garlic when grilling chicken or fish.

PASILLA chilies are one of the most popular chilies. They have an earthy, smoky, long-lasting flavor with mild heat. They are most often paired with ancho and mulatto chili powder.

Herb & Spice Blends

The following herb & spice blends have been used for hundreds of years. They're readily available at your local supermarket and can be used by themselves to season just about any dish.

BOUQUET GARNI is a mixture of basil, marjoram, rosemary, savory, thyme, tarragon, oregano, sage and dill. It works well in slow simmering dishes like soups and stews. Try using it as the main seasoning when baking fish or chicken.

FINES HERBES is a mixture of chervil, parsley, chives and tarragon. It has a delicate flavor and pairs well with lighter flavored dishes. It's a good substitution for parsley when you want a little color, but better flavor.

CURRY POWDER is a blend of many spices, and comes in more varieties than I can count. Since each curry powder uses different spices, they range from smoky, to sweet, to mild and burning hot. Use it to marinate meats and add a little kick to your vegetables.

CHINESE FIVE SPICE is made from cinnamon, cassia buds, star anise, anise seed, ginger, and ground cloves giving it a delightful combination of sweet, warm, cool and spicy. It is very versatile, and works well with vegetables, marinades, and stir-fries.

GARAM MASALA is a Northern Indian style sweet curry blend based on a mixture of cardamom, coriander and black pepper, but it can also include cinnamon, cumin, caraway, ginger, nutmeg and cloves. It is used primarily on vegetarian dishes, but is good with chicken and fish. Add it at the end of the cooking process to preserve its flavor.

HERBS DE PROVENCE is the classic French herb blend. It's a mixture of rosemary thyme, lavender, marjoram, tarragon, basil, savory and fennel. It pairs beautifully with just about any dish. Try it with beef, chicken, in a soup or stock, or with stewed tomatoes.

ITALIAN HERBS is a mixture of oregano, basil, marjoram, thyme, and crushed rosemary. Use it in a tomato sauce or to season chicken and fish.

JAMAICAN JERK seasoning is a combination of chiles, thyme, cinnamon, ginger, allspice, cloves, ginger and onions. Rub it into chicken, or whisk it into a marinade.

ORGANIC NO-SALT SEASONING, Kirkland Brand (available from Costco) is a mixture of 21 spices. It tastes great on chicken, beef, and in vinaigrettes.

Recipes

When I created this book, I approached it from the viewpoint of how I would want the recipes to read. Other diet cookbooks tell you how to make a single serving of a dish. Well who cooks just a single serving of anything? *I* definitely don't want to be in and out of the kitchen all day preparing one meal at a time.

I'd want to cook something, and then eat it for lunch for the next couple of days. To have the ability to open the fridge when I'm busy, and have something readily available to eat.

Most of my recipes serve four people, sometimes more, sometimes less. Simply look at the protein amount and divide it down until it's around 3.5 to 4 oz to determine the number of servings.

I could have broken everything down to exact amounts, but this diet is more than regiment, it's about retraining you to recognize food, to first measure, then eyeball what a serving is and be liberated by it.

We as a society have become conditioned to recognize the things that large corporations manufacture and sell to us as food. One of the best outcomes from the HCG diet is that by cutting out all those awful chemicals and synthetic junk, you'll have re-conditioned yourself to love the taste of food. Real food. You're hormones won't be as far out of whack anymore and will be functioning closer to the way they're supposed to, burning up the calories you eat and not piling on 10 lbs overnight just because they were in the mood.

Turn the page and explore. Use the What & Why section as a resource and the next several pages as inspiration. Dream up combinations of your own and try them out. Sometimes they'll taste just fine, sometimes they'll taste awful, but that's okay because sometimes you'll come up with something that's just so fabulously good that it was worth all the interesting meals that came before it. Dream, explore, have fun and good luck!

-Melissa

Steak, Asparagus & Garlic Tomatoes

Beef

Steak

BEEF DOESN'T HAVE TO HAVE a million things on it in order to taste good. Preparing it simply, with kosher salt and freshly ground black pepper allows the flavor of the meat to shine through. Select a good cut of meat and enjoy.

Steak
Kosher Salt
Freshly ground Black Pepper

Preheat grill to medium-high heat. Spray grill with nonstick, nonflammable cooking spray.

Season the steaks with kosher salt and pepper. Toss on the grill and shut the lid. Let them cook for 4 to 6 minutes per side, or until desired degree of doneness.

Steak Arugula Stackers

ALMOST A SNACK, BUT MORE FILLING. These little hand held bites are great when you want to nibble on dinner while watching TV. A slight cheat to this recipe is to add Horseradish or Mustard. If you use the cheat version, look for brands that don't have oil, and have the least amount of sugar possible, but you already knew that. Right?

Leftover Steak
Arugula
1 Wasa cracker
Horseradish or Mustard
Kosher Salt
Pepper

Break a Wasa cracker into 4-6 pieces. Slice a piece of your left-over steak into thin strips. Layer, the cracker with arugula, steak, and horseradish. Salt & Pepper to taste.

Serve at room temperature.

Spicy Mustard Burgers & Watercress

ALTERNATELY, USE THE SPICES BELOW and turn it into a marinade for a steak. It'll taste yummy.

---

1 lb Sirloin, ground
1 Shallot, diced
1 handful Parsley, chopped
1 dash Cloves, ground
1 T Mustard, powder
1 tsp Chaloula hot sauce
1 small bunch Watercress

In a medium size bowl, fluff the ground sirloin, diced shallot, parsley, cloves, mustard, & Chaloula together with a fork. Once thoroughly mixed, form into patties and grill, bake, or cook them in a skillet.

Serve on a bed of watercress.

Chili Sauced Steaks

WHEN SELECTING A BROTH FOR THE SAUCE, remember to look for a brand that doesn't use MSG or have any added sugar.

Steaks
Kosher Salt
Pepper

SAUCE
1 small Red Onion, minced
2 cloves Garlic, minced
1 T Chili Powder
1 tsp Oregano, dried
2 T Tomato Paste
1 cup Beef Broth
2 dashes Cloves

Grill the steaks, seasoning with salt and pepper to taste.

While the steaks are cooking, heat a few tablespoons of water in a large skillet and sauté the onion and garlic until the onion begins to turn translucent. Season with salt and pepper, then add the cloves, oregano, chili powder, and the tomato paste, then cook for a minute or so.

Stir in the beef broth and let simmer for a few minutes.

Ladle the sauce over your steak and enjoy!

Savory Pot Roast

1 lb Pot Roast, trimmed
  of all fat
6 cloves Garlic, smashed
  and peeled
8 Shallots, halved
½ cup Red Wine Vinegar
Kosher Salt
Pepper

Using a hot skillet over high heat, sear the pot roast on all sides and set aside. Allow the pan to cool slightly and using a few tablespoons of water, sauté the shallots until they begin to brown, then toss in the garlic and cook until fragrant.

Toss all the ingredients and 2 cups of water into a crock pot set to high. Once the water begins to boil, turn the crock pot down to low and let it simmer until done, approximately 2½ hours.

The Well Mannered Steak

A SAVORY DELICIOUS STEAK. The trick with this is to get a good cut of meat. I like to use the Costco cuts that have the ¼ inch of fat along the edge.

---

1 Steak fillet
¼ tsp Marjoram
¼ tsp Thyme
¼ tsp Oregano
2-3 T White Wine Vinegar

While Grilling:
Kosher Salt, to taste
Black Pepper, to taste

Trim all fat, gristle, and other stuff you really shouldn't be eating off the steak. Combine all the ingredients together in a plastic bag, squeeze all of the air out of the bag so the meat won't turn brown, then toss it in the fridge and forget about it for a couple of days. The longer it marinates the better it will taste.

Season the steak with Kosher Salt & Pepper. Place it on a grill heated to medium high, flip once when the steak begins to firm up. Cook until desired level of doneness is achieved.

Enjoy.

Grandma's Meatloaf

IT WASN'T DIFFICULT TO TRANSFORM Grandma's Meatloaf recipe to work with the HCG diet. It was simply a matter of omitting the egg, and substituting bread for a Wasa cracker. Hope you enjoy this recipe as much as I do.

---

1 lb ground Sirloin
1 small Onion, diced
1 stalk Celery, diced
1 tsp Kosher Salt
¼ tsp Poultry Seasoning
¼ tsp ground Pepper
¼ tsp dry Mustard, ground
2 dashes cloves, ground
2 Wasa crackers, crushed
1-2 cups Spicy Ketchup, pg 170

Lightly fluff ingredients together with a fork, lightly press the meat mixture together in the bottom of a bowl to form a rounded loaf, then slide it out onto a foil lined baking sheet.

Pat it into shape once more, then cover liberally with spicy ketchup.

Bake at 350°F for 50 minutes.

Fennel & Onion Meatloaf

IN ORDER TO KEEP YOUR MEATLOAF from turning into a brick, mix it lightly with a fork. You're not so much mixing, as lightly tossing a mixture together. What you want to avoid is mashing the ground sirloin until it becomes a thick, dense log of meat. Keep it airy, keep it light, lift everything together with a fork.

1 lb ground Sirloin
½ bulb Fennel, thinly sliced
½ med Onion, thinly sliced
1 rib Celery, diced
2 T Tomato Paste
2 dashes Cloves, ground
1 splash White Wine Vinegar
2 Wasa crackers, crushed

Thinly slice the onion and fennel into 1 inch long pieces. Sauté the fennel, onion, kosher salt, and pepper with a splash of water in a non-stick skillet until onion becomes translucent. When the fennel and onions have cooled, toss them together with the other ingredients.

Once mixed, lightly press the mixture together in the bottom of a bowl to form a loaf. Slide it out onto a foil lined baking sheet, then re-form into desired shape.

Bake at 350°F for 50 minutes.

Spinach & Chard Meatloaf

SOMETIMES I LIKE TO PUT A PAN OF HOT WATER in the bottom of the oven while the meatloaf is baking, if you're not using a very wet sauce to top your meatloaf, adding a little bit of steam will help keep the meatloaf moist and stop the surface from cracking.

---

1 lb Sirloin, ground
4 cups Spinach, chopped
4 cups Chard, chopped
2 Wasa Crackers, crushed
1 tsp Sage, ground
½ tsp Kosher Salt
½ tsp Pepper
¼ tsp Mustard Powder
¼ tsp Nutmeg
¼ tsp
1-2 cups Tomato Sauce, pg 168

Microwave chopped spinach and chard for four minutes, or until limp. Drain excess liquid and set aside to cool. When the spinach and chard has cooled, mix in remaining ingredients.

Once mixed, lightly press the mixture together in the bottom of a bowl, then slide it out onto a foil lined baking sheet.

Reshape into a loaf, top with the Tomato Sauce.

Bake at 350°F for 50 minutes.

Happy Sloppy Joes

A FUN NEW TWIST ON AN OLD CLASSIC. The ground sirloin really makes this recipe possible. With a fat content of less than 10% it's legal on the HCG diet, which is why these Joes are happy.

---

1 lb Sirloin, ground
2 cups Marinara, pg 169
Lettuce Leaves
Kosher Salt
Pepper

Brown the ground sirloin in a skillet, then drain the liquid and fat when done. Add in 2 cups of marinara sauce, and heat until warm. Salt and pepper to taste.

Serve on lettuce leaves.

Meatballs & Sauce

1 lb Sirloin, ground
2 cloves Garlic, minced
¾ tsp Oregano, dried
1 can (28 oz) Tomatoes, crushed
1 can (15 oz) Tomatoes, whole
Kosher Salt
Pepper

Using a fork, fluff the ground sirloin, oregano, ½ of the minced garlic and 2 tsp of kosher salt together. Then gently form the ground sirloin into 12 meatballs.

In a large pan, over medium heat, cook the meatballs until browned, turning occasionally. Drain the excess oil, then add in the two cans of tomatoes and the remaining garlic and a little pepper. Bring to a boil, then reduce heat and let simmer for about 30 minutes.

Bangladeshi Beef Curry

2 lbs Sirloin, cut into 1½ inch chunks

1 Onion, chopped

6 cloves Garlic, minced

5 Thai Green Chile Peppers

1 tsp fresh Ginger, peeled, sliced, and ground into a paste

3 Cardamom Pods

2 Cloves, whole

1½ Cinnamon, sticks

1 tsp Cumin, ground

1 tsp Coriander, ground

1 tsp Turmeric, ground

1 tsp Garlic, powdered

1 tsp Cayenne Pepper

1 cup Water

In a skillet over medium heat, sauté the onion in a little bit of water until it turns translucent. Reduce the heat to medium-low, and continue cooking until the onion is very tender, about 10-15 min.

Add the garlic, green chilies, ginger paste, cardamom pods, cloves, and cinnamon sticks. Cook until the garlic browns, stirring occasionally.

Add the cumin, coriander, turmeric, garlic powder, cayenne pepper, and water, and then simmer until the mixture has thickened.

Stir in the cubes of beef and cook on medium-low heat, stirring occasionally, until the meat is cooked through and is tender, about 1 to 1½ hours.

Chicken 21 with Apples & Lettuce

Chicken

Lemon & Balsamic Chicken

ADD IN A LITTLE AGAVE TO SWEETEN THINGS UP. After you've moved on to the next phase of the diet add in a some whole wheat spaghetti, a little parmesan cheese, and a few roasted pecans to round things out.

---

2 Chicken breasts, cut into strips

2 sprigs Rosemary, fresh

1 Lemon

¼ cup Balsamic Vinegar

¼ cup Sage leaves, fresh

4 cups Arugula, or baby Spinach

2 generous pinches of Kosher Salt

Pepper, to taste

Zest the lemon, by lightly running a fine grater around the peel, and finely chop the rosemary. Thinly slice the sage leaves by laying them atop one another, rolling them together, then thinly slicing through the roll.

Put the chicken strips into a small glass pan and sprinkle the rosemary, sage, salt, pepper and lemon zest over the strips so that they are evenly coated. Cut the lemon in half and squeeze the juice onto the chicken, then pour the balsamic vinegar in as well. Slice the lemon remnants into smaller chunks then nestle them down around the chicken (after the chicken has cooked, discard them).

Cover in foil and bake at 350°F for 40-45 minutes until chicken is cooked through. Serve hot, over a bed of arugula or baby spinach.

Lime Chicken

1 lb of Chicken, sliced
   into strips
2 Limes, juiced
1 bunch Green Onions
Kosher Salt
Pepper

Slice the green onions, on an angle, into two inch pieces, then set aside.

In a skillet over medium high heat, cook the chicken strips for about three minutes, stirring occasionally. Add the green onions, lime juice, and season with salt and pepper and cook until the chicken is cooked through.

Feisty Chicken

MY MOM NAMED THIS RECIPE THE FIRST TIME she tasted it. I hope you enjoy it as much as she does.

Chicken
Feisty Smoked Rub, pg 156

Sprinkle the Feisty Rub over the chicken until all the surfaces are thoroughly covered, then marinate overnight in an airtight container. The next day grill or bake the chicken.

Slice into strips and serve over a salad.

Chicken 21

I SERVED THIS AT A DINNER PARTY and everybody raved about it. It's so full of flavor that it doesn't register as diet food. The key to this recipe is the Costco 21 spices mix. You'll love it on chicken, beef, steamed veggies, and as the base of a home-made vinaigrette. But be forewarned, it doesn't pair well with fish.

Chicken Breasts
Kirkland Organic No-Salt
   Seasoning
Brown Rice Vinegar
Kosher Salt

In a bowl, sprinkle the Costco brand (Kirkland Signature) organic no-salt seasoning liberally over the chicken, making sure to coat both sides. Add in a pinch of kosher salt per chicken breast, then drizzle brown rice vinegar down over the chicken, until the liquid begins to pool just a little bit. You don't want the chicken submerged, but don't skimp.

Cover the bowl and forget about it for a day or two. Then grill, pan sear, or bake the chicken. My favorite is to grill it.

Chicken Provencal

I'VE MADE THIS RECIPE FOR SO LONG I can't remember when I started. All I know is it's easy to put together and delicious.

---

2 Chicken Breasts
2 cloves Garlic, minced
2-3 T Herbs de Provence

Place the chicken breasts in a small glass baking dish, spread the garlic and sprinkle herbs de provence over both sides of the chicken, then cover with foil.

Bake in a 350°F oven for 1½ hours or until chicken is cooked through.

Garlic & Thyme Chicken

COMFORT FOOD AT IT'S BEST. Enjoy the subtle and mild flavor of this dish. Just a reminder that the larger the garlic piece is, the more gentle the flavor.

---

2 Chicken Breasts

1 medium Red Onion, cut into small wedges

1 head Garlic, cloves separated but left un-peeled.

6 sprigs Thyme

1 Lemon, quartered

2 T Balsamic Vinegar

Kosher Salt

Pepper

Combine all of the ingredients, except the chicken, in a mixing bowl and toss. Place the chicken in a glass baking dish and pour the other ingredients onto the chicken.

Cover with foil, and bake at 400°F for an hour or until chicken is cooked through.

Asparagus & Chicken

THIS RECIPE IS ANOTHER QUICK AND EASY FIX for using up your leftovers. Any type of seasoned chicken will do, from spicy, hot to mild and garlicky. The sky's the limit.

---

2 cups Asparagus, chopped

3 cups Chicken, cooked and cubed

1 cup Cherry Tomatoes, cut in half

½ small Red Onion, diced

1 handful Basil, julienned

Kosher Salt

Pepper

Steam or microwave chopped asparagus until tender crisp. Drain, then set aside. Julienne the basil into thin strips by stacking the leaves, rolling them into a compact bundle, then slicing through the roll.

Sauté the asparagus, chicken, tomatoes and onion in a skillet over medium heat, until warmed through and food is beginning to sear. (Searing happens when the food surface that touches the pan begins to brown.)

Toss in the basil, then salt and pepper to taste.

Cucumber & Chicken Salad

AFTER THE DIET PHASE, add in penne pasta, some extra virgin olive oil, and a little agave for a delicious and filling summer salad.

---

2 Chicken breasts, cooked and thinly sliced

1 Cucumber, English, thinly sliced

10 Radishes, thinly sliced

½ small bunch Cilantro, chopped

1½ Limes, juiced and zested

Kosher Salt

Pepper

Mildly seasoned leftover chicken will work great for this recipe, otherwise, grill or bake 2 chicken breasts with a little salt and pepper.

Toss the ingredients together in a bowl. Season with salt and pepper. Serve with hot or cold chicken depending on your preference.

Tandoori Chicken

UTILIZING ONE OF MY FAVORITE RUBS, this tandoori chicken recipe is a classic that will work for practically any meat. Fish, shrimp, beef, . . . and lamb for when you're off the diet of course. It's versatile, it's simple, and you'll love it!

Uncooked Chicken
Tandoori Rub, pg 158

Liberally sprinkle the Tandoori Rub onto the chicken breast, place them in a plastic bag and marinate in the refrigerator overnight.

Pan sear or grill until done. Serve with salad, cooked spinach or chard.

Tastes great either hot or cold.

Chicken Salad

THIS RECIPE WORKS BEST WITH MILD SEASONED CHICKEN.
By using a mild flavored chicken you allow the salsa to drive the flavor
of the salad. To shake things up a bit, leave out the salsa, add cucumber
and slice in leftover Feisty Chicken.

3.5 oz Chicken, leftover
½ cup Pico de Gallo, pg 120
1 cup Lettuce, shredded
Kosher Salt, to taste
Pepper, to taste

Salt and pepper shredded lettuce,
toss and set aside. Slice the cold
chicken into thin strips, then top the
lettuce with salsa and chicken.

Enjoy!

Desert Lemon Chicken

TO GIVE A LITTLE VARIETY to the recipe, add in ½ tsp. chili powder.

---

2 Chicken Breasts
2 cloves Garlic, minced
½ Lemon, juice
1½ tsp Cumin, ground
Kosher Salt
Pepper

Rub the minced garlic and cumin into the chicken breast, then sprinkle the lemon juice onto the chicken. Set it aside to marinate for 10 -15 minutes, then grill.

Chicken Salad, with Soy Lemon Dressing

HAVE LEFTOVER CHICKEN? Then try out this recipe.

SALAD

1½ cups Chicken, cooked and thinly sliced

½ head Napa Cabbage, shredded

6 Radishes, thinly sliced

1 rib Celery, thinly sliced

¼ cup Mint Leaves, chopped

1 Green Onion, sliced into thin strips

DRESSING

3 T Soy Sauce

2 T Lemon Juice, fresh

1 tsp Agave

Combine the soy sauce, lemon juice and agave in a sauce pan and bring to a boil. Remove from heat and let cool.

In a medium sized mixing bowl, combine the salad ingredients and toss them together with the soy-lemon dressing. Enjoy.

Savory Apple Chicken

2 Chicken Breasts
2 large Shallots, thinly sliced
4 Granny Smith Apples,
   cored and quartered
1 cup Chicken Stock
2 tsp Apple Cider Vinegar
Kosher Salt
Pepper

Place all of the ingredients, except the vinegar, in a glass baking dish. Cover with foil and bake at 350°F for one hour. Remove the foil and continue to bake for 30 minutes or until chicken is cooked through.

Remove the chicken and apples from the baking dish and stir the vinegar into the remaining liquid. Drizzle this pan sauce over your chicken and accompanying side dish.

Chili Garlic Chicken Strips

2 Chicken Breasts, cut into
   thick strips
4 cloves Garlic, diced
¾ cup White Wine Vinegar
½ cup Soy Sauce
½ tsp Red Pepper Flakes
½ tsp Agave

In a non-stick skillet, sear (but not cook) the chicken strips over medium-high heat, then set aside.

In the skillet, sauté the garlic in a little bit of water until fragrant, then stir in the vinegar, soy sauce, red pepper flakes and agave. Toss the chicken back into the pan and simmer, covered, for 10-15 minutes. Uncover and cook an additional few minutes until the sauce has reduced to a thicker consistency.

Cardamom Chicken

2 Chicken Breasts
4 cloves Garlic, crushed
3 T Soy Sauce
2 T Rice Wine Vinegar
2 tsp Agave
¼ tsp Cardamom, ground
¾ tsp Kosher Salt
¾ tsp Pepper

Put all of the ingredients, except the salt and pepper, into a gallon size resealable bag. Place chicken breasts in the bag, and squeeze everything together, to coat the chicken. Press the air out of the bag and seal it shut. Marinate in the fridge overnight or for at least 4 hours.

The next day, discard the marinade and place the chicken on a glass baking dish. Season with kosher salt and pepper, then cover with aluminum foil.

Bake in 400°F oven for 40 minutes, or until chicken is cooked through.

Ginger Lime Tilapia & Bok Choy

Seafood

Ginger Lime Tilapia

SIMPLE, EASY & GREAT TASTING the flavors from this dish reminds me of someplace beachy & tropical. Try this recipe with shrimp to shake things up a bit.

---

2 Tilapia, fillets
1 Lime, zested & juiced
½ T fresh Ginger, finely
    grated
    or ½ tsp Ginger, ground
1 T Mint, julienned
Kosher Salt

Rub the lime zest and ginger into the fish fillets, squeeze half of the lime onto the fish and sprinkle with mint and 2 pinches of Kosher Salt per side. Cover, set aside, and allow to marinate for at least 30 minutes. The remaining mint will turn brown quickly, so put it in a plastic bag (squeezing out all the air) to use later.

Sear the fillets on a hot non-stick skillet, then immediately turn the heat down. Cook on low until the fish flakes apart. Squeeze the rest of the lime over the fish, toss the remaining mint on top. Serve hot.

Serve with Cucumber slices, or if you feel like living dangerously, toss a few baby bok choy in the skillet as soon as you've removed the fish. Add 1-2 T hot water, cover and steam until done, turn once so that both sides become seared and pick up the ginger lime flavor lingering in the pan.

Tandoori Masala Shrimp

THE TANDOORI MASALA RUB IN THIS RECIPE is authentic and fabulous. Make sure to allow the shrimp to marinate long enough to acquire that characteristic tandoori flavor.

Uncooked Shrimp
Tandoori Masala Rub,
    pg 159
Lemon Wedges

Peel and devein the shrimp, leaving the tail on. Sprinkle the Tandoori Masala rub over the shrimp until it's covered evenly. Marinate the shrimp in the refrigerator for 4-6 hours, in a sealable plastic bag.

Remove any excess marinade from the shrimp before cooking, and discard. Thread the marinated shrimp onto a metal or wooden skewer, and grill over medium heat, turning once, until fully cooked.

The shrimp should be browned on the outside but deliciously tender on the inside.

Squeeze fresh lemon over the hot shrimp. Enjoy.

The shrimp can also be cooked on a foil lined baking sheet, in a 400° F oven for 2-3 minutes each side.

Crab Salad

THIS RECIPE HAS A CRISP AND REFRESHING taste and is easy to prepare. Make the dressing ahead of time to save time. The dressing can also be drizzled over fish, chicken, or cooked greens.

Dressing
1 T Brown Rice Vinegar
1 T fresh Lemon juice
1 T fresh Lime juice
¼ tsp Kosher Salt
Pepper to taste

Salad
2 cups Asparagus, chopped
12 oz Crab Meat
1 cup Cucumber, sliced

Mix vinegar, lime & lemon juice, kosher salt and pepper together, set aside. Microwave asparagus until tender-crisp. Drain and set aside to cool. Roughly chop the crab meat, then combine all salad ingredients together, pour dressing over the top, toss, & serve immediately.

Lemon & White Fish

SO SIMPLE YOU'LL WONDER why you've never cooked fish like this before.

---

1 fillet White Fish
Lemon slices
Chives, fresh
Kosher Salt
Pepper

Bring a large pot of water to a boil. On a piece of foil, place the fish fillet, sprinkle a generous pinch of kosher salt over it, freshly grind some black pepper over top, place a few lemon slices on top, then bundle the package up together, taking care to seal the edges by crimping them together.

Toss the foil packet into the boiling water and cook until the fish is firm to the touch, about 10 minutes.

Sprinkle with freshly chopped chives, and enjoy.

Shrimp & Tomatoes

1 lb Shrimp, peeled, deveined and chopped
1 T Cajun seasoning
1 bunch Green Onions
4 Tomatoes
1 head Lettuce
1 rib Celery, diced
2 dashes Cloves, ground
½ tsp White Wine Vinegar

Thinly slice the green onions, separating the white and green part of the onion. In a skillet over medium heat, bring a few tablespoons of water to a boil. Add the shrimp, the white part of the green onion, cajun seasoning, vinegar, and cloves and cook until the shrimp is opaque, about 2 minutes.

Put the shrimp into the refrigerator to chill. Core the tomato and cut each one into eight sections leaving the bottom part of the tomato connected. Place each tomato onto a bed of lettuce and set aside.

In a mixing bowl toss the cooled shrimp, the remaining green onions, and celery together, then spoon part of the mixture into the center part of each tomato.

Spicy Shrimp & Cucumber

2 T Rice Vinegar

1 pinch Kosher Salt

2 English Cucumbers

12 oz Shrimp, peeled, cooked and diced

3 dashes Cayenne Pepper

¼ heaping cup Mint, chopped

Cut the cucumbers into ¾ inch lengths, then hollow out part of the center from each slice, set aside.

In a mixing bowl, combine the vinegar, salt, and cayenne pepper and whisk it together. Add the mint and shrimp, then toss it together. Spoon some of the mixture onto each cucumber slice.

Shrimp & Grapefruit Salad

REFRESHINGLY LIGHT, you'll like the combination of the sweet, subtle citrus and shrimp.

---

1 lb Baby Shrimp, cooked

2 heads Lettuce, Butter Leaf, torn into bite size pieces

2 Pink Grapefruits, peeled, cut into bite size pieces

2 tsp White Wine Vinegar

Kosher Salt

Pepper

When you cut up the grapefruit, save the juice to toss over the salad.

In a large mixing bowl, toss the lettuce, shrimp, and grapefruit together. Then sprinkle the vinegar and the grapefruit juice over top, toss again, then season with kosher salt and pepper to taste.

Apple Poached Fish

2 fillets of Tilapia, rinsed and
   patted dry
2 Braeburn Apples, peeled
   and cored, and sliced
½ small Red Onion, sliced
1 clove Garlic, minced
2 tsp Jamaican Allspice
½ Cup Apple Cider
Kosher Salt
Pepper

Place the sliced apples in lemon water to keep them from turning brown as you cook. In a skillet over medium heat, sauté onion and garlic briefly in a little bit of water, then remove and set aside.

Place the fish fillets on the skillet and brown, then remove and set aside. Deglaze pan with the apple cider vinegar, place the fish, onions and garlic back in the skillet and sprinkle with the allspice. Let simmer for a couple minutes, then add the sliced apples, cover with a lid and let simmer for 6-7 minutes. Salt and pepper to taste.

Serve with steamed vegetables.

Baked Tilapia

2 fillets Tilapia
2 Green onions, cut into
  chunks
4 slices Ginger,
  unpeeled
½ tsp Whole allspice
2 Star Anise pods, broken up
¼ tsp Whole peppercorns
¼ tsp Red Pepper, flakes
Salt and pepper to taste
2 T White Wine Vinegar
½ c Fish or Vegetable Stock

Place the spices, onion, and ginger on the bottom of a glass baking dish. Lightly season the fillets of fish with salt and pepper, then lay the fish on top of the spices. Pour the vinegar and stock into the dish, and then loosely cover with a piece of aluminum foil.

Bake at 400°F for 25-30 minutes.

Tip: Drizzle the broth from the fish over your steamed vegetables or salad.

Mustard Fish

SO EASY it's almost criminal. Simply pick your favorite mustard, or if you're being super strict that day, go for powdered mustard.

White Fish Fillet
Mustard

Spread mustard over the fish fillet, wrap in foil.

Bake in a 400°F oven until the fish flakes apart, about 20 minutes.

Salt Roasted Shrimp

I LEARNED THIS TECHNIQUE FROM Alton Brown when I watched an episode of his show dedicated to salt. The result is shrimp, with an intense, concentrated flavor.

---

4 lbs Rock Salt
1 lb Shrimp, with heads on

Pour the rock salt evenly into two baking dishes. Throw them into the oven, and set the temperature to 400°F.

Once the oven reaches 400°F, wait for 15 more minutes, then put all of the shrimp into one of the dishes. Take the second dish of rock salt and pour it on top of the other, completely covering the shrimp.

Bake for 8 minutes, then check to see if they're done. Shrimp should be pink and opaque, if they're not, return to the oven for another 1-2 minutes.

The rock salt can be reused, simply wash it with hot water, to remove any juices from the shrimp. Then pour it out on a tray and stick it in a warm oven to dry.

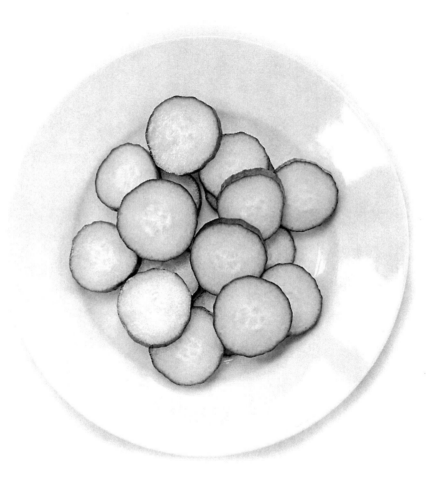

English Cucumber Slices

Vegetable

Pico de Gallo Salsa

I'VE BEEN MAKING THIS SALSA FOR YEARS. It's perfectly suited to a low-fat diet. Full of flavor, light and fresh. It perfectly compliments many dishes and adds flavor when tossed into a salad.

---

2 vine ripe Tomatoes, chopped
½ med. White Onion, diced
½ cup Cilantro, chopped
1 Lime, juiced
1-3 dashes Cayenne Pepper
3 pinches Kosher Salt

Combine all the ingredients and toss. It's as simple as that.

This salsa is great with the Ginger Lime Chicken, the Feisty Chicken, and with the Beef Fajitas. It makes a great mid-afternoon snack when topped on a Wasa cracker.

Beet Greens

SPICY & HOT these beet greens are savory. They're perfect with a lightly seasoned piece of meat.

---

1 lb Beet Greens
½ small Onion, thinly sliced
1 large clove Garlic, minced
1 cup Water
¼ tsp Crushed Red Pepper flakes
Red Wine Vinegar, splash

Rinse the beet greens in cold water, twice. Cut away woody stems and discard. Roughly chop the remaining greens, then in a large skillet over medium heat, cook the onions with a splash of water until soft, then add the garlic and red pepper flakes.

When the garlic and pepper have become fragrant, add the remaining water and toss in the beet greens. Reduce the heat to low, cover the skillet and simmer for 5-15 minutes until tender, then stir in the vinegar.

For kale or collard greens cook for an additional 20-25 minutes until tender.

Roasted Asparagus

ROASTING MAKES THE ASPARAGUS more flavorful and sweet. Sometimes food prepared simply, tastes better.

Asparagus Spears
Kosher Salt

OPTIONS
Black Pepper
Minced Garlic
Balsamic Vinegar
Lemon Juice, fresh

Trim and wash the asparagus spears, place on a baking sheet, season with a pinch of kosher salt and one of the following, chopped garlic, balsamic vinegar, or lemon juice.

Bake at 450°F for 15 minutes. To promote even browning, occasionally shake the pan to roll the spears over. Spears should be lightly browned & tender, but not charred.

Cucumber Mint Salad

COOL AND REFRESHING, use this dish as an accompaniment to fish. When you've begun the next phase of the diet, add in a little plain greek yogurt to shake things up a bit.

1½ English Cucumbers
1 Lemon, juiced
6 Mint leaves, thinly sliced
Kosher Salt
Pepper

Thinly slice the cucumbers, then in a medium bowl combine the ingredients and toss. Add salt and freshly ground black pepper to taste.

Sauerkraut

TOP A BURGER WITH IT. EAT IT HOT or cold. This sauerkraut recipe is as authentic as you can get and it tastes great!

---

5 lbs Green Cabbage, shredded
3 T Pickling Salt
1 T Juniper Berries, dried
2 tsp Caraway Seeds
1 quart Water in a sanitized glass jar

In a large bowl, mix cabbage thoroughly with salt, juniper berries, and caraway seeds, with tongs. If you use your hands, make sure that they are very clean (so that you don't transfer the bacteria from your hands to the soon to be sauerkraut). Let stand for 10 minutes.

Pack the cabbage mixture down into a large plastic food container. Top the canister with a smaller lid so that the lid rests on the cabbage and doesn't seal the canister shut. Rest the glass jar filled with the water on top of the lid.

Leave the container in cool area (65 to 70 degrees F). After a day, the cabbage should have given up enough liquid to be completely submerged. The jar serves as a weight to keep the cabbage submerged and away from air.

Check cabbage every other day for approximately 2 weeks and skim the surface of scum, if necessary. Let stand for 4 weeks. Once done, transfer the sauerkraut to an airtight container and store in the refrigerator for up to 6 months.

Simply Kale

SAVORY & YUMMY, add in some cubed sweet potatoes and olive oil when you're on to the next phase of the diet.

1 bunch Kale
1 dash Nutmeg, ground
1 cup Chicken Broth

As always look for chicken broth without MSG, sugar or chemicals (your best bet is to look for an organic brand).

Wash the kale, then roughly chop it. Heat the chicken broth in a large skillet, then add in the nutmeg and kale. Cover and let simmer until done. If the pan dries out before the kale has cooked, then add in a little more broth.

Coleslaw

PATTERNED AFTER GERMAN coleslaw, this recipe makes a great side for many dishes. In particular, you might try it with pan seared fish topped with Pico de Gallo Salsa. When you make this coleslaw in your post-HCG days, vigorously whisk ½ cup of olive oil into the dressing.

DRESSING
5 T Apple Cider Vinegar
1 tsp Mustard, dry
½ tsp Celery Seeds
Kosher Salt
2 T Agave

COLESLAW
½ head Green Cabbage
1 small head Red Cabbage
½ White Onion, grated

Put the vinegar, mustard, agave and celery seeds into a medium bowl and whisk to combine. Season with salt to taste and set aside.

Core, then finely slice the cabbage. In a large bowl, add the dressing to the cabbage and toss to combine. Store the coleslaw in the refrigerator until ready to use, up to 1 day.

Serve chilled.

Lime Ginger Bok Choy

1 head Bok Choy,
   chopped
2 cloves Garlic, thinly sliced
Kosher Salt
Soy Ginger Dressing, pg 179

Combine the ingredients for the dressing and set aside. In a large skillet, over medium-high heat, bring a couple tablespoons of water to a boil, and then toss in the garlic and sauté until fragrant. Add in the bok choy and season with salt and pepper.

Stir or toss the bok choy frequently while cooking, until it turns bright green. Remove from heat and drizzle the soy ginger dressing on top.

Roasted Tomatoes & Arugula

USUALLY, YOU'D USE OLIVE OIL to not only bring out the flavor of the tomato and thyme, but to help the thyme, salt and pepper stick to the tomato. On the HCG diet, that's a no-no, so we're using water. Work quickly so you can get the thyme to stick.

---

2 cups Cherry or Grape
   Tomatoes

4 sprigs Thyme, de-stemmed

Kosher Salt

Pepper

2 bunches Arugula,
   trimmed

Wash the tomatoes and immediately toss them with thyme, salt and pepper. Place on a baking sheet and bake at 450°F for 15 minutes or until the tomatoes begin to shrink.

Serve the hot tomatoes on a bed of arugula.

Garlic Tomatoes

Tomatoes, vine ripened

Garlic, fresh minced, or
   granulated

Kosher Salt

Pepper

Cut the tomato in half, place the halves on a baking sheet, then sprinkle garlic, salt, and pepper on the cut surface.

Bake at 450°F until the tomato is heated through and the top is beginning to bubble. About 10 minutes.

Roasted Rosemary & Onions

3 Red Onions, quartered
3 sprigs Rosemary, de-
  stemmed and chopped
½ tsp White Wine Vinegar
Kosher Salt

Toss the onion and rosemary to-gether, then place on a baking sheet. Sprinkle 2-3 pinches of salt over the onions.

Bake at 450°F for 10-15 minutes, then using tongs or a spatula, turn the onions over and allow them to cook an additional 5-10 minutes, letting them brown.

Scoop the onions into a serving dish and sprinkle the vinegar on top.

Strawberry Cucumber Salad

THIS SALAD MAKES AN EXCELLENT TOPPING FOR chicken and fish. Simply dice the strawberries and cucumber so that it turns into a pseudo chutney.

---

2 tsp Balsamic Vinegar
1 tsp Mustard, powder
1 English Cucumber, halved and sliced
1 cup Strawberries, sliced
2 T fresh Mint, chopped
Lettuce
Kosher Salt
Pepper

In a medium bowl, whisk together the balsamic vinegar and mustard. Add the cucumber, strawberries, and mint then toss to combine. Season to taste with salt and pepper. Serve on top of whole lettuce leaves.

Apple Cucumber Salad

2 tsp Dijon Mustard

2 T fresh Dill, chopped

3 T Apple Cider Vinegar

2 Tart Apples, like Gala,
Pink Lady or Braeburn,
thinly sliced

1 English Cucumber, thinly
sliced

½ sweet onion, thinly sliced

Whisk the mustard, dill, and vinegar together. Set aside.

Toss the sliced apples, cucumber and onion with the dressing and serve.

Apple Salsa

TRY THIS SALSA WITH BAKED TILAPIA. When you've started the next phase of the diet, try it with mangos instead of apples.

---

1 Apple, diced
1 Green Onion, sliced thinly
½ Lime, juiced
1 large sprig Mint, minced
1 small pinch Kosher Salt
1 dash Pepper

Toss it all together. Use it as a garnish.

Soup

Asparagus Soup

CLEAN AND FRESH. By the time you've completed the first round of this diet, your body will have readjusted. Your hormones will have re-booted and will be working in synch with each other better, much, much better than ever before. If you hadn't noticed already, you're eating fresh, you're eating close to the vine, you're not eating all that processed junk that you used to. Keep this recipe fabulous, by scrutinizing that label on the chicken stock. You want organic, you don't want things you can't pronounce, and you certainly don't want any MSG, a cheap additive that adds flavor but wrecks havoc on your system.

---

2 cups Asparagus, diced

1/2 small onion, diced

1/2 tsp Kosher Salt

1 cup Chicken Stock

Freshly ground Black Pepper, to taste

Using a medium saucepan, sauté the onions in a little bit of chicken stock until soft. Add the remaining chicken stock and the salt. Bring to a boil, then reduce heat. Simmer over low heat until asparagus is creamy and tender. Top with freshly ground black pepper.

Ginger Asparagus Soup

A VARIATION ON A CLASSIC ASPARAGUS SOUP. When you've started the next phase of the HCG diet, try adding in some cellophane noodles (cooked & drained) and a splash of sesame oil.

4 cups Chicken Stock
2 thick slices fresh Ginger
1½ cups Asparagus, chopped
2 Green Onions, thinly sliced
5-6 Peppercorns
2 ribs Celery, sliced
½ Lemon

Bring chicken stock, ginger, peppercorns, and lemon to a boil. Add the celery, then reduce the heat and let simmer for about 20 minutes. Discard the lemon, and add the asparagus. Cook until the asparagus is tender crisp, about 2-4 minutes. Stir in green onions and serve immediately.

Seafood Stew

12 oz Red Snapper fillets,
    skinned and cut into
    1" cubes
1 lb medium Shrimp,
    deveined and peeled
1 clove Garlic, minced
1 bulb Fennel, thinly sliced
1 large Tomato, chopped
4 cups Chicken Broth,
    low sodium
Kosher Salt
Pepper

In a large pot sauté the minced garlic in a couple tablespoons of water until fragrant. Add fennel and cook stirring frequently, until softened. Add more water as needed to keep fennel and garlic from sticking to the pan.

Add the tomato and season with salt and pepper. Cook until the tomato begins to soften, then stir in the chicken broth and bring to a soft boil.

Slide the seafood into the pot and reduce the heat to low. Let the stew simmer gently until the seafood is thoroughly cooked.

Tip: All meats cut more easily when partially frozen.

Chicken Salsa Soup

LEFTOVER PICO DE GALLO SALSA? No problem, make a soup.
When you're on the next phase of the diet, toss in some sour cream and
sliced avocado as a garnish.

---

2 Chicken Breasts, cut into
  thick strips
4 cups Chicken Stock
1 Onion, chopped
6 cloves Garlic, minced
1½ cups Pico de Gallo, pg 120
1 cup Cilantro, chopped
Kosher Salt

In a large pan sauté the onion in a few tablespoons of water until softened, then add the garlic and cook for a few more minutes. Add the chicken and stock and bring to a boil, then reduce the heat and gently simmer for 5 minutes. Stir in 1 cup of salsa, cover the pot, and simmer for an additional 20-30 minutes until the chicken is cooked through.

Pull the chicken out from the pot and shred or cut it into smaller pieces.   Return the chicken to the pot, season with salt, then stir in the remaining salsa and the cilantro. Enjoy!

Pho

I FELL IN LOVE WITH PHO in 2007, and couldn't find a restaurant within walking distance of my apartment (in NYC) to satisfy my cravings. So I ended up making my own. This recipe, sans the rice noodles, is the outcome. Enjoy.

BROTH
2 32 oz boxes Beef Stock
1 Onion, halved
2 inches of Ginger, peeled
3 sticks Cinnamon
10 Cloves, whole
1 T Coriander Seeds
5 Allspice Seeds
3 Star Anise
½ tsp Pepper

SOUP
7 oz Beef, sliced thinly
6 leaves, Napa Cabbage
  sliced thinly
½ cup Spinach, chopped
2 Green Onions, sliced
2 tsp Cilantro, chopped
6 leaves Basil, torn
1 Lime, cut in half
Ground Fresh Chili Paste,
  to taste

In a pot, over medium-high heat, bring the beef stock to a boil and drop in the onion and ginger.

Pan roast the spices, in a skillet over medium heat, until they become fragrant, about 30 seconds. Transfer the spices onto a piece of cheesecloth and tie it shut, then put the bundle into the beef broth. Reduce the heat, and simmer uncovered for about an hour. If the flavor becomes too strong, add a little water. (Discard the onion, ginger, and spices when done.)

While the broth is simmering, prep your vegetables and meat so that they have time to warm up to room temperature. Divide the cabbage, spinach, cilantro, basil, and beef into two large soup bowls, leaving the raw beef on top. Squeeze half a lime over each bowl and discard the rind.

When the boiling broth is ready, ladle it into your bowl. The beef will cook instantly, and the vegetables will blanch. Add in a little ground fresh chili paste (beware it's SPICY), and enjoy!

Moroccan Chicken Soup

A QUICK, YUMMY SOUP using leftover chicken.

---

2 Chicken Breasts, thinly
  sliced, leftovers

1 Onion, diced

5 cups Chicken Stock

1 (14.5 oz) can Tomatoes,
  diced

½ bulb Fennel, sliced

1 cup Spinach, chopped

1 tsp Garam Masala

Kosher Salt

Pepper

2 tsp Cilantro

½ Lemon, juice

Sauté the onion in a saucepan over medium-high heat until slightly browned, then stir in the garam masala and cook until fragrant, about 30 seconds.

Add chicken stock, tomatoes and simmer for 10 minutes. Add in the chicken, then salt and pepper to taste. Top with cilantro and a squeeze of fresh lemon juice.

Crab Soup

1 lb Crab Meat
2 quarts Fish or Vegetable
    Stock
¼ tsp Cayenne Pepper
1 small Onion, minced
1 tsp Lemon Peel, grated
½ tsp Mace, ground
1 T Parsley, finely chopped
1 dash Apple Cider Vinegar
Kosher Salt
Pepper

Bring the fish stock to a boil, then stir in the crab meat, onion, lemon peel, and mace. Reduce the heat to low and simmer, partially covered, for about 20 minutes.

Stir in the vinegar, then add in salt and pepper to taste. Ladle the soup into bowls and garnish with parsley.

Snacks

Wasa Cracker

INTERESTINGLY ADDICTIVE, THESE LIGHTWEIGHT and low calorie crackers make a great snack. Top them with practically anything, it'll taste good.

TOPPINGS
Pico de Gallo Salsa, pg 120
Tomato Sauce, pg 168
Spicy Ketchup, pg 170
Marinara, pg 169
Strawberry Sauce, pg 173

Cinnamon Apple

COLD AND CRISPY, I FELL IN LOVE with cinnamon apples the first time I tried them. I discovered these from a co-worker who wasn't dieting. They're just that good of a treat.

Apples
Cinnamon
Plastic sandwich bag

Thinly slice an apple, put the slices in a plastic bag, then liberally sprinkle cinnamon over them, shaking the bag until all the slices are evenly coated. Refrigerate until the apple is icy cold and the cinnamon's had enough time to seep down into the apple, at least 1 hour.

Enjoy!

Baked Apple Crisp

A FEW BAKING APPLES OF CHOICE are Rome, Pippin, Winesap, Granny Smith, Golden Delicious, Cameo or Gingergold. Any of these will work great for this recipe.

---

2 lbs Rome Apples
1 T fresh Lemon Juice
½ tsp Agave
½ tsp Vanilla
1 tsp Cinnamon, ground
¼ tsp Cloves, ground
1 dash Nutmeg
2 Wasa Crackers, crushed

Core and slice apples. Combine the sliced apples, lemon juice, agave, cinnamon, cloves and nutmeg in saucepan. Cook over medium heat until apples are tender, stirring occasionally, about 13 minutes. Mix in half of Wasa crackers, then transfer the mixture to 9-inch glass pie dish. Sprinkle remaining crackers over the apples.

Bake at 375°F for 30 minutes until the topping is golden brown. Let cool for 10 minutes before serving.

Harvest Apple Sauce

MIX & MATCH YOUR APPLES FOR A ROBUST TASTE or stick to one variety to bring out the one flavor. There are hundreds of varieties of apples, one of my most recent favorites are Honey Crisp.

---

4 lbs Apples
1 T fresh lemon juice
2 T Agave
1 stick Cinnamon

Peel, core and cut the apples into large chunks, tossing them with the lemon juice to prevent discoloration. Put the apple mixture into a pan and bring to a boil. Reduce the heat to a simmer, cover partially, and cook until apples are very tender, about 15 minutes. Uncover the pot and cook 5 minutes more.

Remove from heat and discard the cinnamon stick. Mash the apples into the desired consistency, allow it to cool, then refrigerate.

Applesauce will keep for 5 days.

Vanilla Strawberry Crisp

YUMMY, YUMMY TO YOUR TUMMY. A healthy twist to a decadent dessert. In the next phase of the diet, add a dollop of whipped cream.

FILLING
8 cups Strawberries
2 T Agave
1 Wasa Cracker, crushed
1 T Lemon zest
2 T Lemon juice
1 tsp Vanilla

TOPPING
2 Wasa Crackers, crumbled
1 T Agave
½ tsp Cinnamon, ground
1 tsp Vanilla
Pinch Kosher Salt

Remove the green leaves from the strawberries and discard. Slice the strawberries into bite size pieces and place in a mixing bowl. In a separate bowl, combine the crushed Wasa cracker, agave, lemon zest & juice, and vanilla. Mix well. Then pour the mixture over the strawberries and gently fold together. Place the strawberry mixture in a glass or ceramic baking dish.

Mix the topping ingredients together and sprinkle over the strawberries.

Bake at 350°F for 45 minutes, cool slightly before serving.

Radish Toppers

ON THE NEXT PHASE OF THE DIET substitute the Wasa cracker for a piece of whole grain buttered bread.

---

15 radishes, shredded
¼ cup Dill, chopped
1 Lemon, zest
¼ tsp Pepper, ground
Kosher Salt, to taste
Wasa Crackers

Toss the radish, dill, pepper and lemon zest together in a bowl, then season with kosher salt. Pile it on a Wasa cracker and enjoy.

Baked Apple

BAKING APPLES, Golden Delicious, Granny Smith, or Winesap. Sure they taste great uncooked, but they become more delicious when baked.

---

1 Apple
½ tsp Cinnamon, ground
¼ tsp Agave

Core the apple, then cut into quarters. Place the apple on a sheet of foil, then sprinkle the cinnamon and agave over the top. Wrap the foil together to enclose the apple inside. Place on a ceramic or glass baking dish.

Bake at 350°F for 15 minutes or until apple is tender.

Strawberry Chard Crisp

WHEN SELECTING THE CHARD FOR THIS RECIPE, look for chard with thicker stalks.

1½ cups Chard stems, sliced
1 cup Celery, sliced
2 ½ cups Strawberries, sliced
3 T Agave
2 Wasa crackers, crushed
½ tsp Lemon zest
½ tsp Lemon juice
½ tsp Cinnamon, ground
1 tsp Vanilla
¼ tsp Kosher Salt

Wash the chard, cut off the leafy part of the chard and save to eat later. Slice the stems into ½ inch lengths, do the same with the celery. Cut the strawberries, into chunks and slices.

Set aside half of the crushed Wasa cracker, then combine the rest of the ingredients in large bowl. Toss gently to blend. Put mixture into a glass baking dish, sprinkle the remaining Wasa crackers on the top, then cover with tinfoil.

Bake at 375°F for 45 to 50 minutes, or until it starts bubbling, then remove the foil covering and bake for an additional 10 minutes until golden brown.

Rubs

Feisty Smoked Rub

THIS IS MY MOTHER'S FAVORITE RUB. It's great when paired with chicken! The spanish paprika and chipotle chili powder are what give this rub its smoky flavor. The arbol and cayenne pepper are what make it feisty.

---

1 T Kosher Salt
1 T Pepper
1 T Chipotle Chile, powder
1 T Spanish Paprika
1 tsp Cinnamon, ground
1 tsp Ancho Chili, powder
1 tsp California Chili, powder
1 tsp Cumin, ground
1 tsp Coriander, ground
1 tsp Garlic, granulated
1 tsp Onion, powder
1 tsp Ginger, ground
1 tsp Cloves, ground
1 tsp Fennel Seed, ground
1 tsp Allspice, ground
1 scant tsp Chili de Arbol, powder
½ tsp Cayenne Pepper

Store in an airtight container.

Fennel Rub

PAIR IT WITH chicken, beef, or fish.

1 cup Fennel Seeds
3 T Coriander Seeds
2 T White Peppercorns
3 T Kosher Salt

Roast the fennel seeds, coriander seeds, and peppercorns in a skillet over medium heat. Shake the skillet frequently to help the seeds toast evenly. When they become fragrant pour them out onto a plate to cool.

When the spices have completely cooled, use a blender to turn them and the salt into a fine powder. Store in an airtight container.

Tandoori Rub

THIS SPICE RUB works well with chicken, shrimp, & fish.

---

1 T Ginger, ground
1 T Cumin, ground
1 T Coriander, ground
1 T Paprika
1 T Turmeric
1 T Salt, Kosher
1 T Cayenne Pepper

Store in an airtight container and close the lid tightly after use.

Tandoori Masala Rub

THIS SPICE RUB works well with chicken, shrimp, & fish.

---

1 tsp Garlic, powder
1 tsp Ginger, powder
1 tsp Cloves, ground
1/2 tsp Nutmeg, ground
1 tsp Mace, powder
1½ T Cumin, ground
2 T Coriander, ground
1 tsp Fenugreek, powder
1 tsp Cinnamon, ground
1 tsp Black Pepper, ground
1 tsp Cardamom, ground

Store in an airtight container and close the lid tightly after use.

The Smoky Rub

IT'S THE SPANISH PAPRIKA THAT GIVES THIS RUB it's smoky flavor. With two different chili powders to give it just enough heat, and the herbs and mustard to round it out, it tastes great!

---

1 T Ancho Chile Powder
2 T Spanish Paprika
1 tsp Oregano, dried
1 tsp Coriander, ground
1 tsp Mustard, dry
1 tsp Cumin, ground
1 tsp Kosher Salt
½ tsp Pepper
½ tsp Chile de Arbol

Rub it on a steak, mix it into a burger, toss a little on your fish & chicken.

Make an impromptu vinaigrette out of it with fresh lime juice and a bit of white wine vinegar, you just might be surprised at how good it turns out.

Baby Back Special

USUALLY USED ON RIBS this rub works great on chicken and beef.

3 T Hungarian Paprika
2 T Red Pepper Flakes
1½ T Onion, powder
1½ T Garlic, powder
1½ T Basil, dried
1½ T Mustard, powder
1 T Kosher Salt
2 tsp Thyme, dried
2 tsp Ginger, ground
½ tsp Pepper

Sprinkle generously over your meats and let them marinate for a bit before you throw them on the grill or in the oven.

Store in an airtight container.

The Spanish Rub

TRY IT WITH CHICKEN or beef, or you could sprinkle a little of this on your steamed greens.

---

6 T Spanish Paprika
2 T Cumin, ground
1 T Mustard, powder
4 tsp Fennel Seed, ground
4 tsp Pepper, ground
2 tsp Kosher Salt

Whisk together and store in an airtight container.

Toasty Cinnamon Rub

TRY IT ON SHRIMP, chicken or to flavor some sautéed spinach.

¼ cup Fennel Seeds
1 T Coriander Seeds
1 T Peppercorns
1½ tsp Red Pepper Flakes
¼ cup California Chili, powder
2 T Kosher Salt
2 T Cinnamon, ground

Toast the fennel, coriander and peppercorns in a skillet over medium heat, shaking the pan frequently to promote even toasting.

Once the spices become fragrant, add in the red pepper flakes and shake the pan side to side for a few seconds. The red pepper flakes will toast quickly and might make your eyes water, so work quickly to heat them up, then scoop the seeds and flakes out onto a plate to cool so you can run out of the room and find fresh air.

Once everything has cooled, puree the fennel, coriander, peppercorns, and red pepper flakes in a blender until the spices have turned into a fine powder. Once finished, pour the powder into a mixing bowl and stir in the chili powder, salt and cinnamon.

Store in an airtight container.

Bay Seafood Seasoning

WHEN SEASONING CRAB, mix this rub 50/50 with Kosher Salt.

---

1 T Bay Leaves, ground
2½ tsp. Celery Salt
1½ tsp Black Pepper
1 tsp Hungarian Paprika
1 tsp Mustard, ground
¾ tsp Nutmeg, ground
½ tsp Cayenne Pepper
½ tsp Cinnamon, ground
½ tsp Allspice, ground
½ tsp Ground Clove, ground
½ tsp Ginger, ground
¼ tsp Mace, ground
¼ tsp Cardamom, ground

Combine all ingredients in a bowl.
Store in an airtight container.

Italian Seasoning

THIS SEASONING BLEND IS VERSATILE, use it in stews, soups, in a marinara, salad dressing, meatloaf, or to season beef or chicken.

---

2 T Basil, dried
2 T Marjoram, dried
2 T Oregano, dried
2 T Thyme, dried
2 T Rosemary, dried

Store in an airtight container.

Sauce

Tomato Sauce

MORE THAN JUST A SAUCE this is a very mild marinara that will compliment just about any dish, from beet greens to pan seared white fish.

---

8 Tomatoes, vine ripened
1 small Onion, diced
2 Garlic cloves, diced
1 rib Celery, diced
½ tsp Kosher Salt
½ tsp Pepper
1 Bay Leaf, whole

In a pot over medium-high heat, sauté the onions and garlic in a few tablespoons of water until the onions are translucent, about 10 minutes. Then add the diced celery and cook another 10 minutes. Add water when necessary to keep the food from sticking or burning.

While the onions, garlic, and celery are cooking, dice three of the tomatoes and set aside. Cut the remaining 5 tomatoes into quarters then blend in a blender until smooth. Add the tomatoes, salt, pepper and bay leaf, then simmer uncovered over low heat until the sauce thickens, about 1 hour. Add more salt and pepper to taste.

Marinara

I LOVE THIS MARINARA AS A TOPPING on Wasa crackers, but there is so much more to it than that. With it's classic Italian flavor, it works great with chicken and fish dishes, and brings flavor to steamed greens.

---

1 med Onion, chopped
2 cloves Garlic, minced
1 can Crushed Tomatoes (28 oz.)
1 tsp Oregano, dried
1 tsp Basil, dried
1 tsp Marjoram, dried
2 small Bay Leaves, whole
Kosher Salt
Pepper

Over medium heat, sauté onion and garlic in a few tablespoons of water until the onions begin to turn translucent. Add the tomatoes and stir. Add in the herbs, salt and pepper, then lower the heat and simmer uncovered for 45 minutes, stirring occasionally.

Spicy Ketchup

THIS RECIPE IS WELL WORTH THE EFFORT. Although painstaking (you have to baby sit this for a couple hours) this is one of the best homemade ketchups you'll ever taste.

---

1 lb Plum Tomatoes
1 lb canned Plum Tomatoes, make sure they don't have added sugar
2 brown Onions, chopped
½ bulb Fennel, chopped
1 rib Celery, chopped
1 inch piece Ginger, sliced
2 cloves Garlic, sliced
¼ tsp Red Pepper Flakes
1 bunch Basil
1 T Coriander, seeds
2 Cloves, whole
Kosher Salt
1 tsp Black Pepper, freshly ground
¾ cup Red Wine Vinegar

In a large pot over low heat, sauté the fennel, onion, celery, ginger, garlic, red pepper flakes, basil stalks (save the leaves for later), coriander seeds, black pepper, cloves, and a large pinch of salt.

Cook slowly for 10 to 15 minutes, stirring often, until the vegetables have softened. Add the tomatoes and 1½ cups water. Bring to a boil, then reduce heat, simmer until the sauce reduces to a thicker consistency.

Add the basil leaves, then puree the sauce a little at a time in a food processor or blender. If you use the blender, blend slowly and in short bursts, otherwise you'll burn yourself when the lid blows off.

After it's blended, using a rubber spatula, push the ketchup through a fine mesh strainer so that it becomes smooth and shiny. Be careful not to burn yourself.

When finished, put the sauce back into the pan and add the vinegar, then let the ketchup simmer until it gains the desired consistency. Stir occasionally.

Curry Ketchup

THE INGREDIENTS IN THIS RECIPE ARE BLENDED AT THE beginning instead of the end. So mince the garlic and onion as small as you can, and make sure when you puree the tomatoes that they're smooth as you can get them.

---

6 Roma Tomatoes
2 lbs Tomatoes, vine ripe
1 small Onion, diced
1 tsp Tomato, paste
1 clove Garlic, minced
2-3 tsp Curry Powder
½ tsp Mustard, ground
½ tsp Ginger, ground
1 dash Cayenne Pepper
2 dashes Cloves, ground
1 pinch Cinnamon, ground
¼ cup Apple Cider
   Vinegar
Kosher Salt

Quarter the tomatoes, then blend in a blender or food processor until smooth. Set aside.

Sauté the onion in a couple tablespoons of water over medium heat until softened but not browned. Add all the ingredients except the vinegar and salt, bring to a boil, then reduce the heat letting the mixture simmer for about an hour. Stirring occasionally.

Add the vinegar, then cook for an additional 30 minutes or so until the desired consistency is reached, then add the salt to taste.

Steak Sauce

THIS RECIPE IS A BIT OF A CHEAT, since most ketchups have sugar, and so does the Worcestershire sauce, but it's good.

---

1 Onion, chopped
1 large clove Garlic, smashed
½ tsp Allspice, ground
½ cup ketchup
½ cup Worcestershire Sauce

In a pan, over medium-high heat, simmer the onion, garlic and all-spice together until the onion is softened. Using a food processor or blender (be careful of the hot steam!) puree the mixture.

Return the puree to the pan and stir in the ketchup and Worcestershire sauce, then simmer over low heat for about 5 minutes or until the sauce has thickened to the desired consistency.

Strawberry Sauce

PUT IT ON A Wasa CRACKER, top your fish or chicken, eat it decadently with a spoon. You'll love this easy to make sauce.

1½ lbs Strawberries
1 Lemon, juiced
1 T Balsamic Vinegar

Trim the strawberries so they're free of stems and leaves. Slice and chop them into random sizes. Then in a medium saucepan, mash the strawberries together with the lemon and vinegar. Cook over medium-high heat until softened, about 3-4 minutes.

The Fish Dipping Sauce

---

2 T Rice Wine Vinegar
2 T Soy Sauce
1 Green Onion, thinly sliced
½ tsp fresh Ginger, grated

Mix it all together. Serve immediately.

Enjoy.

Dressing

Balsamic Mustard Vinaigrette

THIS IS A GREAT DRESSING FOR both chicken and beef. It's simple to make and is tasty. For post HCG life, substitute the powdered mustard for your favorite mustard and whisk in 1½ cups of Extra Virgin Olive Oil a little at a time.

½ cup Balsamic Vinegar
2 T Mustard, powder
Kosher Salt
Pepper

Pour the vinegar into a bowl. Whisk in the mustard. Season with kosher salt and pepper. You can also add minced shallots, fresh herbs, citrus zest or crushed red pepper.

Refrigerate in an airtight container for up to two weeks.

Soy Ginger Dressing

DRIZZLE IT OVER STEAMED GREENS or your favorite fish. This Asian inspired dressing will add lots of flavor.

¼ cup Soy Sauce

3 T Lime Juice, fresh

½ tsp Agave

1 tsp fresh Ginger, finely grated

Mix together and serve. May be refrigerated in an airtight container.

Lemon Tarragon Vinaigrette

DURING THE NEXT PHASE OF THE DIET when it's okay to use oils, whisk in 1½ T Olive Oil before adding the tarragon. Drizzle this dressing over roasted asparagus, salad greens, or white fish.

1½ T Lemon Juice, fresh
1 Shallot, minced
1 T Tarragon Leaves, fresh
1 tsp Mustard, powder
Kosher Salt
Pepper

Whisk the lemon juice shallot, and mustard together, then add salt and pepper to taste, then stir in the tarragon.

Drinks

Savory Citrus

FOR THOSE TIMES YOU WANT TO FEEL LIKE you're in Provence. Serve this drink when company comes over, or treat yourself on those days when you just want to sit outside and watch the world go by. It's a pretty sight in a glass pitcher.

---

1 gallon Water
3 small sprigs Rosemary
1 Lime, sliced
1 Orange

Slice the peel off the orange into spirals, discard the inside. Place the orange peel spirals, sliced lime and rosemary sprigs into the water and let steep for a few hours. Best served chilled.

Citrus Slush

½ cup boiling Water
½ tsp Agave
1 tsp grated Lemon Peel
¼ cup Lemon Juice, fresh
½ tsp grated Lime Peel
¼ cup Lime Juice, fresh
2 cups Ice Cubes
4 leaves Mint, fresh

Blend the boiling water, agave, grated lemon peel and lime peel together in a blender. Add the lime juice, lemon juice, and ice cubes and blend for a few seconds, then toss in the mint leaves and blend until the mixture is slushy.

Cucumber Mint Slush

3 cups Water
4 cups Ice Cubes
2 Cucumbers, peel one,
    and cut both into chunks
¼ cup Lime Juice, fresh
½ tsp Agave
1 sprig Mint, fresh

Using a blender, puree the cucumber, water, agave and mint together, then slowly add the ice until it's blended smoothly together.

Serve with a slice of lime as a garnish

Limeade

I FELL IN LOVE WITH LIMEADE IN GUATEMALA. Limes are plentiful in Central America, and are used to flavor everything.

6 Limes, juiced
1 T Lime zest
2 T Agave
3 cups Water
1 sprig Mint, fresh

Bring 1 cup of the water and the lime zest to a boil over medium-heat, remove from heat and allow it to cool.

Once cool, strain the lime zest from the liquid using a fine mesh strainer and stir in the rest of the water, the lime juice, agave, and mint. Chill, or serve immediately over ice.

Index

We'd love to hear from you.
Tell us which recipes are your favorites
and what you wish we'd written more about.

Have a success story you want to share?
We'd love to hear it.

Drop us a line @
HCGfeedback@daedalianpress.com

Did you find this cookbook helpful while on the
HCG diet? If so, please write us a review at
at Barnes & Noble, Amazon.com or
wherever you purchased the book.

Thanks much & best wishes!

LaVergne, TN USA
24 February 2010
174129LV00004B/60/P